Shine Your Light

Dedicated to my husband, Keith, and our wonderful journey of life together ...

And with thanks to all who shared their journeys and trusted in the therapeutic process. I trust you will continue to shine your light ...

Shine Your Light

How to Increase Your Self-esteem and Lead Your Best Life

SUSAN MALONE-HOYLE

THE CHOIR PRESS

First published in the United Kingdom in 2024 by

The Choir Press

ISBN 978-1-78963-451-8

Contents

Introduction

This book is not only about my own personal journey of low self-esteem/life experiences, but it is also about other people's experience of working on this issue within therapy, sharing approaches, techniques and an opportunity to complete worksheets to see their own progression and change. The main aim of this book is to provide hope to those of you who have experienced various difficulties when having low self-esteem and to show that there is a way to overcome these challenges. Not all of my experiences are shared as it was more important to share some of my experiences regarding the subject matter and the labels given than to give the reader the whole story of my life. This book is about low self-esteem from my own perspective, although I have researched the subject along the way. Following and implementing research as well as trying to make sense of this complex topic, my aim is to share some of my personal journey as to why I had low self-esteem, what action I took to increase my self-esteem and how, by increasing my self-esteem, my life completely changed. Also, giving others an idea of what it was like for other people attending therapy to share their experiences and their journeys of low self-esteem.

I share the experiences that shaped me into the woman I am today but also challenging these experiences and finding my own voice. Showing how continued practice of affirmations, challenging negative self-talk, changing old behaviours, changing or getting rid of labels and having positive self-talk can benefit you and those around you. How certain triggers can continue to compound your low self-esteem, how the impact of having higher self-esteem can not only change your life in a positive way but can positively impact on your health, your relationships and your work. Having higher self-esteem can also change the way other people respond to you.

I share what it is like to grow in self-esteem, for me personally, being able to be me (my authentic self), not worrying about what others think of me or allowing others to tell me who I am. Learning how to embrace the love and success that I began to have in my life without feeling I had to give an excuse or be sorry for being happy/successful. I hope that people who read this book find it helpful and manage to practise the exercises to improve their self-esteem. It can work, it does work, but it only works if

you practise as, with practice, things, situations, life can change until eventually these new ways become your natural way of being.
Good luck x

My Philosophy

We can change; we can learn to accept the past and not allow our negative experiences to continue to impact on our future. We are not our experiences. They are just that – 'experiences'. I believe all human beings, given the right support, can improve their circumstances and have a successful, happy life if they choose.

We create our thoughts, and we can change them. We can let go of old labels and we can be the person we want to be. We are not our labels or our experiences. We are responsible for our lives, our futures and the futures of our children.

Self-acceptance and self-love are the key to positive change. We are all good enough, no matter what.

All the people who have shared their experiences in this book have given their permission. All people involved have read and approved of the written experiences before going to print. I have changed most of their names to give them anonymity.

Chapter One

MY JOURNEY (an overview)

My light was dimed as a child, which led to wanting to help others find their light and shine it brightly. Through work on self and life experiences, I found my light again and continue to shine it brightly ...

I was born the youngest of six children into an Irish immigrant family. It was the 1960s, Brixton, South London, and I lived my childhood in poverty. There were no expectations of me as a female except to become a wife and mother in adulthood as that is what women did back then, or at least that is how it was for females within a working-class community. I was not encouraged to achieve at school or otherwise as it was a time when women were mothers and wives looked after the house, their husbands and children. If the women did work, it was generally in factories, shops or domestic work; not that there is anything wrong with that as my mother was a domestic help for many years, but for me it is more about explaining that there were no choices or opportunities given to people in those circumstances, or at least that is how I felt.

As a child, I was told that I had contracted the polio virus and was extremely ill, which led me to having all sorts of tests and hospital experiences. This also led to me feeling as though I was the odd one out in my family dynamics as I was the sickly, poorly one who started school late and who, especially in the early days, was quite dependent on my mother. I found it difficult to do sports and be active, especially with the lack of mobility in my legs. This led to loneliness and isolation during the early years.

I had some good early school years as I had a couple of great teachers who encouraged and could see I was keen to learn. My confidence and education dipped in adolescence when I had the experience of bullying and was teased for being poor, having freckles and just basically deemed as ugly. I received many labels and was called names, which made me feel as though I was not good enough. I struggled throughout secondary school and finished without completing any exams as my negative experiences led me to just want to leave school, so that is what I did. I had experienced a sexual assault by a man when I was sixteen years old, which led me to feel a huge amount of shame and for which I blamed myself for many years. This experience, as well as previous ones before, compounded my lack of worth and kept my low self-esteem going to the point where I went on to blame myself for all of my negative experiences until I was in my early thirties, when things began to change. I have had lots of negative experiences in my life, including various experiences of abuse – psychological, sexual and physical – and have learnt over time to forgive and work through the pain of those experiences. Being born in 1960s London and in poverty, it was my experience that girls/women were treated disrespectfully as second-class citizens. It was a time of children receiving abuse on a daily basis – hit, punched, kicked or caned, and adults normalised this behaviour, calling it discipline. Children did not have a voice, nor were they heard, and were often threatened if they tried to speak out. Children were also left to their own devices; my interpretation was this was due to them being something you just had rather than thought about. In those days, the message I heard was just to get married, have kids and that is your life sorted! There was not necessarily a thought of can I afford them, what do they need? I was told often in my life, 'This is just how it is.'

Due to life experiences, wanting to be independent and not having a secure, safe place in life, I moved from place to place and got involved in relationships that were both harmful and destructive. Due to my lack of worth, it took time for me to realise that I was keeping my low self-worth going by what I was doing and how my lack led to more lacking. I had a belief that I was not worth much so did not even try to achieve anything until employers started to praise me and value my work. This changed my path to success. Once I started to get recognised and was encouraged to go to college, which I did in my early twenties, and then on to university at a later time, my belief began to grow. I initially gained my self-worth from my work and doing for others but gradually over time learnt to grow my esteem from within, but firstly I had to understand healthy boundaries, assertion, self-care and self-nurturing.

My healing came by learning to do some reparative work for myself, teaching myself how to take care of me, exploring what I liked and did not like. There was a complete process of learning, which took me right up until my early/mid-thirties to realise as I learnt how to become more aware of my cycles of behaviour and continued to make mistakes to incorporate changes.

It was both painful and challenging, with many forms of therapy, including talking therapies, acupuncture, meditation, body work and spending time in silence. I went on a journey of discovery to find out who I was without the labels, gradually peeling them off one at a time and looking underneath and behind the masks of trauma, abuse, pain, shame and self-harm. I remember looking at a picture of me at around two to three years of age, seeing the trauma in my eyes and observing how I felt about that moment. Really finding empathy and compassion for me and wanting to give me nothing but love/care/safety right in that moment. I have not looked back since as whenever I look at that photo, which I now keep on my dresser, I feel nothing but love and just want to always cherish that part of me.

I blame my parents for none of the above or for their part in my experience as they had their journeys too. But it was about them taking responsibility for my experience and hopefully learning from that. I have forgiven them for their lack of knowledge regarding parenting and can make sense of the whole experience today.

Becoming a counsellor and going through rigorous training, as well as years of therapy, also allowed me to learn about the woman I am. My journey into counselling started in 1998 and is something that was initially very hard but gradually supported my awareness and further changes to continue my development and personal as well as professional growth. Specific courses in particular addictions training allowed me to understand my family dynamics and the impact on self.

As a therapeutic tool, I may ask some people I work with to write a letter to their younger selves. It allows us to let go of the past, whether it be guilt/shame or something else that is holding us back. It is important to find compassion and understanding for our younger selves, and forgiveness. I encourage you to write that letter as an exercise to help let go of feelings that may have become destructive.

My letter to self:

> Dear Sue (the name I had as a child/teen),
> I know it has not been an easy journey and at times it has felt that you became lost. No matter how hard life appeared to be, you never gave up and you always had love in your heart. You have always believed in the good in others and strived to do your best to be kind. I understand the times when you were not so kind to others and your anger, particularly in your adolescence and teenage years, which was due to your own difficulties at home as well as past trauma. I know that you have felt bad about some of the behaviour you displayed, particularly at school, but it is important to forgive yourself and empathise with your situation at that time.
>
> You are still that sensitive girl who cares about others, and I value that in you. No matter what negative experiences you have had, you still have hope in humankind treating people with respect and love. I understand your past behaviours, your difficulties and love you just the way you are. You are a survivor and did the best you could do to survive the most difficult of situations.
> Your compassion, love, strength, confidence and drive to survive have been things I value in you and always will. I want to tell you I love you today, all of you, just as you are.
>
> Your experiences are just that there is nothing to be ashamed of or to give yourself a tough time about. Keep smiling and keep being you.
>
> I love you x

Letter to self – What would yours say ...?

Chapter 2

SELF-ESTEEM AND THE ORIGINS AND CONSEQUENCES OF LOW SELF-ESTEEM

It is important to get an understanding of what self-esteem is as it is often confused with confidence. We can be high in confidence and low in self-esteem. This chapter explains what self-esteem is, the consequences of low self-esteem, and the origins and importance of self-esteem. I have also added worksheets throughout this book for you to complete so that you can gain a better understanding of where your self-esteem is and the impact of low self-esteem on your life.

What is self-esteem?

Self-esteem is a judgement about our own personal value – the degree to which we believe ourselves to be worthwhile, which also has an impact on our feelings and behaviours.

Although self-esteem can change from day to day, it usually stays within a narrow range; however, sometimes a significant event causes us to re-evaluate our worth.

What do we mean by low self-esteem?

Self-image
Self-concept
Self-perception
All of the above refer to the overall picture a person has of themselves. These terms do not necessarily imply any judgement or evaluation of the self; however, they simply describe a range of characteristics (see below).

- Social, professional, parent
- Life stage: child, grandparent, etc.
- Physical appearance: small, with brown eyes
- Likes/dislikes: I like swimming; I dislike football
- Regular activities: I play netball; I go to cookery classes

- Psychological qualities: I have a sense of humour; I lose my temper easily

Self-confidence/self-efficacy

'Self-confidence' and 'self-efficacy', on the other hand, refer to our sense that we can do things successfully, and perhaps to a standard. For examples, see below.

- Specific: I am good at maths
- Social relationships: I am a good listener
- General coping ability: I am a good person to turn to in a crisis

Self-acceptance/self-respect/self-worth/self-esteem

Self-acceptance, self-respect, self-worth and self-esteem introduce a different element.

They do not simply refer to qualities we assign to ourselves, whether negative or positive. Nor do they simply reflect things we believe we can or cannot do. Rather, they reflect on us as people. Their tone may be positive (I am good) (I am worthwhile) or negative (I am bad) (I am worthless). When the tone is negative, we are talking about low self-esteem.

Self-esteem and behaviour

In general, high self-esteem leads to self-affirming and constructive behaviours; low self-esteem leads to self-defeating behaviour.

Sources of self-esteem:

You control your self-esteem. Nobody else decides how you feel and think about yourself.

(The above is not meant as a blaming sentence.)

It is just that you have come to the beliefs honestly and sometimes painfully from your experiences.

Some of the consequences of low self-esteem:

- May not achieve certain goals in life
- May have little value in your worth, therefore more vulnerable to abuse from others
- More likely to experience abuse, domestic violence, bullying, etc.
- More likely to experience drug abuse, alcoholism, eating disorders, etc.

- More likely to get involved in crime or become a victim of crime
- More likely to allow others to abuse you and take advantage of you due to the lack of value in self
- More likely to feel that you do not have a purpose in life
- May have difficulties in knowing or having healthy relationships
- May not apply for the work that you want but undervalue yourself to do what you think you deserve, which is usually dependent on how low self-esteem is at the time
- May tend to put others before self – most if not all of the time
- May struggle with nurturing of self
- May lack self-care
- May not succeed in taking time and space for self
- May deprive self of hobbies or doing things you enjoy
- May not be living the life you want to live due to the feeling of being undeserving

Origins of low self-esteem

- May have had critical parents/caregivers/guardians
- May not have had achievements recognised
- May have received negative labelling form adults/teachers (low expectations)
- May have had too many expectations put on you then criticised for not achieving
- May not have received nurturing by parents/caregivers/guardians
- May have felt undervalued and not praised or affirmed
- May have been given or perceived as having a negative self-image (told you are ugly/stupid, etc.)
- May have a feeling of being unloved
- May have experienced abuse
- May have experienced neglect or felt neglected
- Being fostered/adopted as a child may have left you feeling as though you are not wanted or do not fit in

Parents/guardians/your perception and experience of the world can give you a negative image, as well as the messages given, e.g., fatty, ugly, told you are no good, etc.

An observation to show how holding a central negative belief about oneself reverberates on all levels, affecting thinking, behaviour, emotional state and body sensations. Consider how this may apply to you.

Resentment, criticism, guilt can keep us all trapped in a place of being victims. I do not believe people who have had negative experiences are victims; they are survivors, people who go through hardships and survive them. One of the things that can impact on our self-esteem is also being addicted to substances as well as having experienced trauma as these too can affect your decision-making and choices as well as esteem.

If you were observing yourself today, what would you see?

What would be the tell-tale clues of low self-esteem in your case?

The importance of self-esteem

Self-esteem reflects the opinion we have of ourselves, the judgements we make and the value we place on ourselves as people. Low self-esteem means a poor opinion of we, judging ourselves unfavourably and assigning ourselves with little worth or value. At the heart of low self-esteem lie our negative beliefs. These can be seen in how we operate daily and can have a considerable impact on all areas of our lives. The role of self-esteem varies. It can be an aspect or a consequence of current problems or vulnerability factor for an entire range of difficulties. Whichever role it occupies, the extent to which it disrupts daily life varies from person to person.

The importance of self-esteem is to acknowledge that all humans make mistakes; therefore, the importance of compassion for self is such as to be able to move forward and have a more contented, fulfilled life.

Low self-esteem is a common issue for most people; however, some people have also had trauma, addiction, abuse, neglect, bullying or lacked nurturing and praise. Recognising achievements daily can enhance and improve esteem. Acknowledging and recognising the small steps taken each day, the journey you have travelled on your own path as an individual and not comparing yourself to others will indeed begin to raise your value of self.

This book will hopefully allow you to be able to explore and challenge your negative thought processes and identify the behaviours that go with them, as well as allow you to move forward and acknowledge that there are choices available to you. Giving you the ability to explore new creativities, knowing that you are unique in your own right as we all have things that we are good at and enjoy. Building a structure, giving yourself a purpose, maintaining a healthy relationship with food, having a regular exercise routine and time for relaxation will all improve your self-esteem.

Valuing ourselves allows us to not only achieve our goals but have the relationships/friendships we deserve to have. Appreciating ourselves for who we are and how we are, connecting with ourselves on a spiritual level can enhance our own value and belief of self.

Being open to new opportunities, challenging yourself more, letting go of old fears/ anxieties that have been holding you back and feeling more able to state how you feel without the need to apologise will allow you to be free to live the life you choose to live, as well as appreciate yourself for who you are.

Everything needs to be on a step-by-step basis, going at the pace that is right for you. Choosing what is useful and what is not. Identifying your path and the steps that you will take to improve and acknowledge the importance of self-esteem in your life. Taking the time to find out what works in your life and how you can implement the changes on a regular basis to support your long-term goal of higher self-esteem.

WORKSHEET

Complete the following exercise to get an idea of how your self-esteem is currently.

When answering the questions below, please answer yes, no or sometimes.

Part one

1 My experience in life has taught me to value and appreciate myself.

2 I have a good opinion of myself.

3 I treat myself well and have good self-care.

4 I like myself.

5 I appreciate my qualities, skills, assets and strengths.

6 I give myself time and space.

7 I am as entitled to other people's attention and time as they are to mine.

8 I deserve the good things in life.

9 My expectations of myself are no more than my expectations of others.

10 I am kind and encouraging towards myself, rather than self-critical.

Highlight the number of statements that are true to you.

1 I have specific goals that I want to achieve.

2 I enjoy doing things for myself without the need of encouragement or praise.

3 I feel able to express my true emotions.

4 I enjoy doing my own thinking and making my own decisions.

5 I can admit to mistakes or defeats without feeling shamed.

6 I can take differences of opinion without feeling upset, angry or wrong.

7 I can accept a gift or compliment without feeling I must explain or give something in return.

8 I can laugh at myself without feeling degraded.

9 I feel free to express my opinions and convictions even when they differ from those of others.

10 I can be alone and not feel isolated.

11 I can let others be right or wrong without feeling I must correct them.

12 I can appreciate and enjoy the achievements of others without comparing myself to them.

13 I can tell a story about myself without tending to brag or build myself up.

14 It is important that I connect with others.

15 I welcome new challenges and face them with confidence.

16 I take responsibility for my own actions without blaming the circumstances or other people.

17 I make friends easily and naturally.

18 I tend to trust other people.

19 I can identify my strengths.

20 It does not bother me to ask for assistance when I need help.

21 I tend not to worry about what the future holds.

Negative or positive self-image creates self-fulfilling prophecy.

To grow in esteem and develop a positive self-image, you need to begin to:

- Value honesty
- Establish healthy boundaries
- Recognise changes and achievements with affirmations
- Work through shameful feelings

Claim your right to be in the world

- Respond appropriately to others
- Acknowledge your vulnerabilities
- Affirm yourself and others

To help you grow in self-esteem, it is important to begin to let go of:

- Dishonest behaviour
- Criticism of self and others
- Recognising when in a role of the victim, a rescuer or an aggressor
- Making excuses for unhealthy behaviour
- Impulsive or compulsive behaviour
- Striving for perfection
- Comparing self to others
- Relationships that are abusive or destructive

The key to transforming low self-esteem has two parts. The first part is through initially acknowledging that your self-esteem is low, and the second part is to sufficiently rebuild self-esteem. To enable this, it is important to make use of the fundamental tools identified below.

- Having a basic structure to the day

- Following your structure (challenging old patterns of behaviour that are unhelpful)

- Having an overall plan for the week which includes support, recreation, family/friends, exercise, rest, relaxation, quality time with self (meditation, affirmation and journalling)

The second part is concerned with the dialogue we have with ourselves. High self-esteem is maintained through feeling yourself to be an effective and relevant human being.

If your inner dialogue with yourself is constantly saying, *You are stupid … That was a horrible thing to say … Nobody wants to know a person like me … I cannot do anything well …* then poor self-esteem is guaranteed.

If you want to have good self-esteem, it is important to work to ensure the dialogue you have with yourself is of a positive nature. No more putting yourself down! This may initially feel hard or uncomfortable, because change always is! But over time and with practice, as well as patience, habits will begin to change.

WORKSHEET

Identifying Changes

At the end of each day –
Reflect on your behaviour, attitudes and responses to others as well as acknowledging how you felt within that process.

Ask yourself:

• Was I defensive today?

• Did I do any acts of kindness today?

• Did I respond appropriately?

• How did I feel about my interactions with others?

• How did I feel others interacted with me?

• How am I doing?

• Why am I grateful?

• What am I grateful for?

It may be useful to keep a daily journal to record your reflections. Acknowledging your progress and identifying areas you still wish to improve upon.

Once you have completed the worksheets, take a look at the answers you have given. Be honest with yourself about your findings. Take time to explore what has led to the answers you have given, taking into consideration how you may have felt on that day, and for the first year at least completing them every three to six months to see if the scores are changing.

Examples of high self-esteem

Being open to criticism, acknowledging mistakes, being comfortable with giving and receiving compliments. People with high self-esteem are unafraid to show their curiosity, discuss their experiences, ideas and opportunities. They are comfortable with social or personal assertiveness.

People with high self-esteem:

- appreciate themselves and other people

- enjoy growing as a person and finding fulfillment and meaning in their lives

- can be creative

- make their own decisions, conform to what others tell them to be and do so only when they agree

- see the world in realistic terms, accepting other people the way they are while encouraging them towards greater confidence and a more positive direction

- can easily concentrate on solving problems in their lives

- have loving and respectful relationships

- know what their values are and live their lives accordingly

- speak up and tell others their opinions, calmly and kindly, and share their wants and needs with others

- act assertively without experiencing any guilt and feel at ease communicating with others

- avoid dwelling on the past and focus on the present moment

- believe they are equal to everyone else, no better and no worse

- reject the attempts of others to manipulate them

- recognise and accept a wide range of feelings, both positive and negative, and share them within their healthy relationships

- enjoy a healthy balance of work, play and relaxation

- accept challenges and take risks to grow and learn from their mistakes when things do not go to plan

- handle criticism without taking it personally, with the knowledge that they are learning and growing and that their worth is not dependent on the opinions of others

- value self and communicating well with others, without fear of expressing their likes, dislikes and feelings

- value others and accept them as they are. Based on the above, we can produce good examples of what high self-esteem looks like.

WORKSHEET

- Write down one positive point to your personality and begin the process of reinforcing this quality.

- Write down a time when you felt able to nurture yourself. For instance, a good night's sleep, healthy eating, exercise, time for self, etc.

- Write down a time when you felt that you had self-belief.

- Write down five things you know that you can do and at which you are good.

- Begin to plan to reinforce your positive qualities ...

Chapter 3

MANDIE'S JOURNEY
(Mandie–female, forties)

I cannot do anything without a drink! That was the panicked voice in my head when the hangover was bad. I would get up and go downstairs and, as soon as possible, I would slip a vodka into my drink. A familiar pattern of behaviour had begun again ... get drunk, drink through the hangover and repeat ... sometimes for days.

For the last six years, I have been running a pub, so the environment I am in made it easy for my behaviour to be acceptable and almost ignored. I never had to look far to find someone with bigger problems than me. I knew I had an issue with alcohol before taking on the pub and had already been referred by my GP in 2009 for six counselling sessions with the AMS (Alcohol Misuse Service), which had helped identify the extent of the problem. I had been able to have periods of abstinence, and after those sessions I had been sober for eighteen months. However, this drinking pattern was repeated several times by me throughout my life. I would be able to abstain, think I had changed and start drinking again, and eventually it would get out of control, so I would stop again.

This time, things were different. Now I had a good life to lose, but I could not stop drinking, and the feeling I would get after a binge was devastating - it was beyond miserable. I would physically ache with disappointment and shame. I was now behaving like someone I would stop serving and kick out. It was humiliating, and I was drowning. Then, one morning, I came round and was terrified. I tried to walk, and pain exploded through the confusion like never before. Coming round and having a bump or bruise had become common as the binges were frequently causing blackouts - the consequences of which usually involved my partner refusing to speak to me for forty-eight hours, and me desperately trying to piece together what I had done or said to whom, and how to repair the damage. This time was serious ... no amount of vodka was going to get me through this shift ... I could not walk. I had broken a bone in my leg and seriously dislocated my ankle, and had no memory of how. (My partner watched what happened on the pub's CCTV, but it is something I could never bring myself to watch.) I spent the day sobering up and trying to work out what to do next. I did not yet know the extent of the injury. It was two weeks before Christmas, the busiest time for us in the pub trade. I could not walk so I could not work. I was in crisis and needed help. If this was not rock bottom, it was as close to it as I wanted to get.

Within days, I had contacted a local counsellor who referred me to Susan, and feeling numb, useless and alone, I began this journey. I found Susan to be a warm and calming influence straight away. She gently guided me along a frightening but fascinating path. I could not figure out why I drank the way I did. I had spent years justifying it, but nothing ever sat right. Nobody has a perfect life, but I had a loving family, was in a long-term and secure relationship and had no real excuse for my behaviour. I had enough self-confidence, education and life experience to know that this was putting everything in jeopardy and had to stop. Susan walked alongside me as I identified myself as an alcoholic, which was the first step. Once I did that, it became something I could own ... it became mine. Not tied up with anyone or anything else ... this was all about me!

The journey took me to the issue of self-esteem and showed me I had extraordinarily little. The problem was that people saw me as a self-confident person who could command authority, run a pub and carry myself through life. But I had no self-value ... no sense of what I am worth. The dissatisfaction and anxiety this caused was what triggered the self-destructive drinking behaviour. Rather than alleviating the negative feelings, it became a vicious circle ... I feel worthless, so I shall hurt myself, so I feel terrible and prove to myself I am worthless ... and so it went on ... from the age of fourteen till forty-one ... a destructive pattern of self-harm. I found out from my partner the true extent of the horror of the blackouts. After becoming spiteful, I would end up consumed by a darkness so emotional that he referred to me as a wounded animal, inconsolable. Although I did not remember, there were flashes of knowing when he shared this with me, and I realised I had been chipping away at myself for a long time, but now it was so self-destructive. When I was able to identify this as the cause of my drinking, I was again able to own it ... and if you own something, you have the right to change it, to deal with it, and that is what I did.

I started to address the uncomfortable relationship I had with myself. Susan encouraged me to start taking care of myself more. It sounds easy, but it meant I had to adjust my way of thinking and consider myself worth taking care of. I was able to care for those who were important to me, so I knew I was capable. But it needed time in the safe, non-judgemental environment that counselling provided, a lot of homework and a weekend self-esteem course that Susan facilitated for me and others to change the deeply ingrained beliefs that I was not of any real value.

This entire process was difficult. I had to step out of my comfort zone, and being vulnerable is terrifying, but the rewards are worth it in the end. I began to see myself differently, to appreciate my strengths and the potential I had to be someone I liked, not just tolerated. Susan's belief was that I would not only like and value myself but learn to love myself. I thought this was a bit much, to be honest! But I was surprised when over the last year of the two years I spent on this journey, I did indeed learn my true value and became conscious of how much my self-esteem needed to be grown as well as be nurtured. From this grew a calmness and acceptance, which made me more likely to respond than react to the world, and this created far less anxiety. I developed new behaviours and gained the tools I needed to maintain those behaviours. In time, this allowed me to become a better version of me ... one I liked; a better partner, daughter, sister, friend, and a far better landlady to my customers. By understanding my relationship with alcohol, I was able to reconcile the difficulties I had being both an alcoholic and a landlady, but that is another story.

As a publican, you are in the spotlight all the time ... everything you do is judged by others and everyone has an opinion. My front door is the front door to the pub ... I would have to walk through the crowded bar straight after a session with Susan, raw and vulnerable. That was difficult. The customers wanted to know where I had been. What on earth could be more important than serving them alcohol on a Friday evening? Ironic really ... At the beginning, I would make excuses and go upstairs and hide in bed, reflecting on the session and wondering how I was going to climb back out from under this mess I had made of my life, until I could put on a smile and do my job. I had to fake it, but it was a means to a wonderful end. The work I have done on myself now means that because I am authentic and honest with myself, my behaviour is something I can be proud of. That does not mean I do not make mistakes, but it means I am able to have a confidence I have never had before. I do not need to fake it anymore. I no longer make excuses and I do not need to explain myself ... I am the sober landlady! Although the journey was coming to a natural conclusion, the pandemic abruptly ended our sessions. This left me with Susan as an anchor if I needed her, but on my own, as everyone was, in a sea of uncertainty. To shut up a pub with no clear end date was worrying, but I had the new improved me for company. At the time of writing, I have been abstinent from alcohol for 1,169 days. I am happy. I love the person I have become. My journey has been difficult, but not just for me. I pushed those who love me too far, and it has taken a long time for them to trust that this period of sobriety will last. I understand that and have had to be patient. They had to get used to this person I have become, and I am indescribably grateful to them. I am now someone I can be proud of. I am now therefore loved more by myself and others. I have grown into an independent, successful woman.

Susan is responsible for changing the lives of many clients, but she is the only counsellor that has made such a profound and lasting difference to me. I have made these changes while running the pub, unable to hide from my demons but forced to face them every day. With improved self-esteem and a mantra of 'Thing by thing' rather than 'Day by day' (a lot can happen in a day), I no longer live a life governed by anxiety, fear and self-doubt. I found it useful to visualise my alcoholism as an entity, a thing, which fluctuates depending on whether I am having a good or difficult day. A force that I will always need to keep in check. I now have the tools to do this. The voice telling me to drink shouts the loudest, not when I am in a social situation or under pressure, but when I am alone ... it really is all about me. I nurture and respect my self-esteem and recovery. They are mine and I embrace them. This takes a lot of energy. Every day, I check them, never wanting to take them for granted and become complacent. Complacency is where the alcoholism gets it strength from, and I am not letting it take control again. I have come full circle and now I can do anything without a drink.

Working alliance

On meeting Mandie, I was surprised by her knowledge and experience of addiction. However, I noticed how separated she appeared from this, seeing from the outside. She was very aware of herself and the behaviours that led her to seek out counselling but not very aware of how to acknowledge, or should I say not very willing to acknowledge, her behaviour as an addict. Mandie informed me of her thoughts about addiction/alcoholism and how she struggled with the term. It was clear to me by her behaviours towards herself that there was a lack of respect and value. However, this was something I encouraged Mandie to explore rather than come from me. We explored her behaviour towards herself at length, and Mandie began to realise how she could approach things differently. We looked at her value, self-esteem and confidence that she already had. Mandie was both open and engaging throughout our work together and always inquisitive about why and what next, which I found intriguing. I really enjoyed working with her quick mind, keen enthusiasm and drive to be the best version of herself. She appeared both open to challenge and to challenge me, which I respected and valued in our working alliance. It was not always an easy journey, and there were times when we appeared to struggle with each other's perception of a situation. However, we talked things through and owned each other's part in our miscommunication, which led the relationship to grow stronger, and there was an acknowledgement of humanness about it. Mandie is still sober today as I write these words, and she keeps me up to date with her sobriety every now and then, which I value and appreciate.

Mandie's case was an unusual one for me as someone who had previously worked in twelve-step residential rehab for years. As her career choice, this would be a 'No'. Working with an alcoholic publican in sobriety could almost appear comical. When talking to my supervisor at the time, this was something unheard-of. The question was, how can I support someone to maintain sobriety while working and living in a pub? Well, I realised this person was unique, as we all are; however, it was her drive to maintain as well as keep herself sober and her determination and ability to not only understand herself and her situation but also to want to do this that made me believe she could.

We went on a journey of discovery which led to Mandie not only beginning to like herself but eventually growing to love herself, which in turn enabled all unhelpful behaviours to cease. It all sounds so simple, and it is not; it is the client's willingness to explore, trust and be open to challenge and be challenged that leads to such a positive ending. Mandie was ready to go on this journey and she had prepared herself for it; she was ready, willing and able. The relationship was one of two strong women with equal respect for each other and value of each other's experiences.

Addiction

The next few pages are a brief overview of addiction and the impact on self-esteem.

As soon as a person begins to become intoxicated, they cause damage to their brain. The brain is incapable of detoxifying alcohol, so once the liver's capacity has exceeded, alcohol starts to loosen up and disrupt normal communication signals in the brain, worsening memory. That is one of the reasons we like it – to forget our worries.

People with addiction issues may engage in behaviours that become compulsive and often continue these behaviours even though the consequences are harmful. When people first begin using drugs/alcohol, it increases their self-confidence. They may become less concerned about what other people think of them. The individual begins to rely on these substances to cope with life. The lack of self-worth can keep people trapped in addiction. This can keep people in a cycle of self-destructive behaviours and self-harm.

People who have low self-esteem may turn to drugs/alcohol to numb the pain and escape everyday life. They may see drugs/alcohol as a temporary release from suffering, bad feelings and problems they are having. They may see drugs/alcohol as the only way to escape or block their pain, which is not permanent. The person addicted may then become more incapable of overcoming the challenges that originally made them want to use the substance. As their addiction worsens, their self-esteem will start to reduce and become less.

What was once an issue of low self-esteem has now turned into an addiction to drugs/alcohol and life that is spiralling out of control.

Some people with low self-esteem hold themselves as being incapable in one or more areas in their lives. They may feel unable to maintain control and, because of this, they could easily find themselves dominated by others, who they perceive as more capable or powerful. Drugs/alcohol may seem to help them, so they continue to use. Eventually, they develop tolerance, then dependence, then an addiction. Their feelings and the problems still exist and may even be worse, especially when they have an addiction.

When using substances to gain higher self-esteem, individuals often begin to rely on these substances to cope with life. Many people want to better understand drug/alcohol abuse causes. Outside of the physical realm – like the increased tolerance that leads to addiction – one may ask, what makes a person turn to drugs/alcohol in the first place?

The answer to the above question can vary from person to person. However, one answer that many have agreed upon is low self-esteem. Self-esteem is defined as the value of one's worth. This type of self-respect plays a crucial role in the likelihood that a person will abuse drugs/alcohol, which in turn means that drug/alcohol abuse treatment needs to be a programme to combat and improve the factors that influence low self-esteem.

When a person has low self-esteem, they may be more influenced by the world around them and their resulting actions. For example, a person with low self-esteem may have trouble overcoming negative thoughts or feelings and therefore turn to outside experiences or activities to change those negative thoughts into positive ones. Drugs/alcohol can be one of the outside activities they turn to in a negative situation or state of mind.

Low self-esteem can lead to lack of development and/or a tendency towards drugs or alcohol consumption. This is just one example of the many studies that have discovered some type of connection between low self-esteem and drug/alcohol abuse.

It is important to understand, however, that in many cases, there is not necessarily a direct connection between low self-esteem and addiction. There can be many other factors that play a role in drug/alcohol abuse causes, such as family history, genetics, other mental or behavioural disorders, etc.

It makes sense that improving self-esteem can have a positive impact on a person who is recovering from addiction. Since low self-esteem can be a contributing factor among drug abuse causes, resolving one of those causes can help. In fact, many drug abuse treatment programmes are designed to address some of the conditions and disorders that affect self-esteem, such as depression, anxiety and other mood disorders.

There are a variety of factors that are the cause of drug/alcohol abuse/addictions and circumstances – not just one. Improving low self-esteem can help combat most common drug/alcohol abuse causes, but it is something that needs to be done as part of a treatment programme.

Chapter Four

SHARLEEN'S JOURNEY
(Sharleen–female, thirties)

My childhood was very chaotic; both parents had alcohol addictions though my mother's addiction was more severe. My dad was what they call a functioning alcoholic, whereas my mum is chronically dependent.

The first six years of my life, our home was above a pub which my parents managed until it became apparent that my mum had to move from that environment due to her addiction. My mum has never been maternal and when my parents ended their relationship, myself and my siblings chose to live with my father. We did not see Mum on a regular basis though when we did have a weekend visit, she neglected us and put us in dangerous situations whereby we witnessed a lot of violence. At times, we had to be escorted home by the police in police cars. I was a scared little girl.

Throughout school, I had experienced bullying both verbally and physically due to me having ginger hair. At times, it was horrendous. I was tiny for my age, had pale skin and wore glasses and was regarded as poor. All these things made me a target. School life was tough, home life was tough, and I believed everything the bullies said ... that I was ugly, my hair was horrible, I was a midget and a tramp. The list goes on ...

I do not think I ever had self-esteem and have struggled with it my whole life. I did not know how to be or how to behave. I was frightened a lot. When my dad met someone new and remarried, he had more children, which resulted in me and my other siblings feeling pushed out and unloved. I got very depressed and in my last year of school during my exams, I attempted to take my own life. The aftermath of that made me leave the family home at the age of sixteen.

I started a health and social care course at college. I was very shy and nervous, giving presentations, and practical work for first aid was a very daunting experience that caused me to have a huge amount of anxiety. I hated everyone looking at me. I would get my words muddled up and say things wrong, which made my anxiety escalate.

I had hoped at that stage that I would become a paediatric nurse or nursery nurse as after years of looking after my siblings from an early age, it was all I knew how to do.

My mother dropped a bombshell that year, drunkenly telling me that the man I thought was my father was not my real dad. The worst part of that was I had to tell him as he did not know either. My world crumbled. I did not speak to my mother for a long time after that as I felt out of place and that I did not belong anywhere.

I found myself in a relationship with an older man about nine years my senior. He controlled my life; things became very toxic. We later had a son, and it was then he became verbally, physically, sexually and emotionally abusive. He tried to ruin my relationships with my family and friends. I became an emotional wreck, feeling worthless and abused. It took a lot of courage to get out of the relationship. With the help of my dad, I managed to do this but felt absolutely broken. I had always said that I would not follow in my mothers' footsteps and be with a man like that, let alone stay with one.

I spent a long time single after raising my son on my own but later went through a promiscuous time and another toxic relationship. He loved a good party and I felt as though I had missed out while raising my son. He drank a lot daily and smoked weed as well as taking narcotics on weekends. He made me laugh, but that and partying was all that held us together. I started to drink more than ever, dabbled in narcotics too, and he became a womaniser, constantly messaging other women, usually saying inappropriate things, also flirting with others while we were out together. He did not stop when I asked him to; he did not see that he was causing me harm. We separated a couple of times due to his behaviour. I became obsessed with changing myself; hair, losing weight. I did not feel good enough. We got back together, and nothing changed. I would bring alcohol every weekend, but the final straw was when he was trying to cheat. As I was good to him, I helped him get back on his feet while in the relationship, so I ended it.

I was always putting others first as it felt rewarding to help others. I could not see that it was me that I needed to help. For the next few years, I slowly spiralled out of control. My son was now fifteen/sixteen; he did not need me as much. I serial dated, drank every weekend, changed jobs and developed an alter ego. She was everything I was not: confident, life and soul of the party, loud, over sharer, took risks, did not care, very sexual. I was in self-destruct mode, putting myself in dangerous situations sexually/emotionally and would self-harm in many ways.

I began counselling with Susan after I lost my driving licence for drink driving. Even though I had hit rock bottom and felt enormous shame and guilt, it did not stop me drinking or binging at weekends. My alcohol use began to affect my son, resulting in him needing some time away from me where I had totally lost myself.

We had always had a good relationship and it hit me hard that he needed to be away from me. I attempted to control my drinking a few times but could not manage this long enough as the consequences were always bad.

It took me two years working with Susan, with her help and support, to realise and admit I was an alcoholic. My final straw was another suicide attempt, and I knew I was sick and tired of being sick and tired.

I am now seven months sober as I write this and am attending AA meetings along with working the twelve-step programme with a sponsor. I finally see my worth and have finally gained some self-respect, facing my demons head-on with the support of the fellowship and Susan. I am working on my self-esteem now that I am in a better place. I need to love myself first. I trust Susan will help me get there. I instantly liked her; always warm, friendly, welcoming, and more importantly, I feel safe.

Working alliance

When working with Sharleen, I knew that she had to find her own way to abstinence and make that decision herself. I was willing and open to working with her, whatever her decision was about her alcohol use.

Sharleen had experienced many difficult things in her life and just needed a safe space to be able to express herself and her needs without judgement.

One of the first things that I noticed initially about Sharleen was her fiery personality and courage as well as her amazing hair, lots of wonderful freckles and a sense of humour.

Sharleen fully committed herself to the process of therapy even though at times I am sure I did not always meet her expectations, nor did I always give her what she wanted or tell her what she wanted to hear. In the early days, there appeared to be some barriers between us. Those certain feelings in particular shame blocked the therapeutic process. She stated in one session that she felt judged, and we explored this at length, whereby she came to realise this was not the case. Having had the experiences she had, I know how much I wanted her to feel at ease and listened to and heard. She had lots she wanted to say, and I said to myself that if nothing at all comes from this, I wanted her to feel and be heard. We had many laughs and struggles with our understanding of each other as well as expectations. I knew I wanted to support her on her journey but realised early on that we had a long way to go for her to gain trust in me and to feel safe working with me. We did not always have weekly sessions. In fact, the sessions became more sporadic for a while and then as Sharleen became abstinent, more consistent. She challenged me and often did not take on board suggestions or encouragement but did things her way, sometimes with negative consequences, but I remained patient and valued this struggle. She had to be and do what she felt was right at that time. Some situations were risky, but again we all need to learn from experience to make changes, and Sharleen was someone who was open to challenging herself as well as learn from her experiences.

When working with Sharleen, she showed me that even when she laughed at things that seemed tragic this was her way of showing how she coped, not always wanting to be a victim of her circumstance but a survivor of her experiences. We have laughed a lot within sessions as well as challenged each other, which I valued. Meeting each other as adults and sometimes as children of addicts who have their own wounds healing. I found her to be courageous, smart, responsible and kind. Still able to show love and care for others even when she may not have always received it for herself.

Chapter Five

SELF-CARE AND SELF-ESTEEM

When we talk about self-care, what do we actually mean?

How do you care for you?

Here are the basics below:

Sustenance, i.e., food and drink. Then there is having the right amount of sleep, implementing the right amount of exercise, as well as motivation to manage your day/days, bathing, appearance, hair, shaving, wearing nice and comfortable clothes, planning for the day, structure, fun, relaxation, time for self, nutrition, eating habits, meditation, organisation skills, etc.

Being kind to yourself by doing something you feel is special (something you like but may not need) because you deserve it, e.g., a nice healthful meal, new clothes, an activity, body maintenance, healthy ways of being, creativity, meditation, time for self, etc.

Self-love, kindness to self/others, self-praise, respect for all including self, commitment to self and having a good support network.

It is important to monitor your emotions when connecting them with caffeine/food/alcohol/smoking/vaping, etc. As human beings, we tend to use the above to cope with life, manage our emotions/stress, etc. By monitoring how you use substances to avoid feelings, fill the space or distract, you will then be more aware of your pattern/s and therefore support change in building a healthier relationship with these substances or decide to abstain. Once we gain an understanding/awareness of the above, this will enable change, healthier patterns of behaviour and healthier life choices.

Eating times and nutrition

Eating regular meals helps not only with energy, clearer focus and balance but also maintains good mental health. There has been a lot of proven research around nutrition and mental health, proving how a lack in our diet can have a negative impact on us. Dr Patrick Holford (writer of

Optimum Nutrition For the Mind) has authored many books and spent years researching the impact of nutrition on our mental health.

It is important to allow yourself at least twenty minutes' break for each meal. This enables good digestion but also gives a feeling of good self-care and being kind to self. Valuing yourself enough to take the time to nurture self. Whether it is three regular meals or six meals a day, it is important to find out what is best for you, what suits you, taking the time to cook, think about nutrition and the food you like to eat. Also perhaps try some new dishes or things that you have not eaten before; try to be experimental and have fun.

What we eat can have an impact on how we feel. Guilt, anger, negative self-talk.

Did you learn to feel loved by eating sugary high-fat foods or what is known as comfort food? Are you someone who eats for comfort?

Does this food make you feel good or negative about yourself?

Is it useful for you or not?

Think about how you feel when you eat certain foods. Do you see them as a treat or a trigger to negative emotions?

So many people say, 'I deserve this cake because ...' then, after they have eaten the cake, criticise or berate themselves into feeling bad! Why? Whatever the issue, there is a reason. If we had self-esteem, we would treat ourselves better, kinder, be more aware of our health and less harmful to ourselves.

Treating ourselves with kindness

We are often so busy living our lives or just doing that we appear to struggle to think about how we talk to ourselves, treat ourselves and what actions we are taking. Spending time with self and just being in that moment is important. We are not always aware of our actions, for instance, not having breakfast, jumping out of bed, rushing breaks, not taking breaks. How we treat ourselves, I believe, will impact on how we feel and how we treat others. When I wake up, I make a cuppa and take it back to bed. I then use mindfulness to prepare myself for the day, before commencing a routine of meditation, exercise, breakfast, work, regular breaks, regular food, walk and sometimes an afternoon nap. All of the above are utilised and considered when booking appointments for the people I work with. Being kind to me, reminding myself of positive self-talk, sometimes reassuring self-talk depending on how the day is going; all impact on my day and others around me. Reminding myself of my qualities, being grateful for my life, praising myself when things go right, reassuring myself when things do not go to plan. Loving and accepting myself for just being me (human).

Exercise

The latest statistics show us that exercising for thirty minutes five times a week improves our metabolism, self-esteem and general wellbeing. This can be in the form of walking, swimming, cycling, jogging, the gym, etc. Exercise improves not only physical wellbeing but mental wellbeing, and there are many statistics to prove this. It does not have to be set exercises although for some they may be the best route. It can be roller skating, ice skating, dancing, body popping, the gym, swimming, salsa, anything that you enjoy and that you feel motivated to do.

Exercise is an important part of self-esteem because it improves our value of ourselves and enables better self-care = self-love. Valuing ourselves to the degree which we deserve. Increasing serotonin levels, improving mood and building esteem.

Sleep/meditation/time for self

It is important to gain an understanding of your own sleep pattern and what hours you need. This does not mean what is usual or what you are accustomed to but what you need. How we do this is by sleeping without the alarm one night a week, monitoring the time you go to sleep to what time you wake up. This can vary from time to time due to tiredness but usually stays within a narrow range. We are all individuals and therefore our sleep pattern will be individual.

Meditation and mindfulness are useful tools to reduce anxiety, improve sleep, improve general wellbeing and much more. If it is something you find challenging, it is a good idea to start with short one-minute body scanning. This will give you an idea of how you feel in your body and the tensions you might hold. You can then build from there and over time get to a place where meditation is a regular state of being daily or every other day over time. Meditation and mindfulness help us live in the here and now, ground us and allow us to get a sense of our feelings as well as our wellbeing.

It is common, especially for parents/caregivers, to struggle with the concept of being available for self. This does not have to be an hour a day but hopefully you can build up to that. Time for self helps with anxiety, stress, the digestive system, self-esteem, relationships with others, anger issues, general overall wellbeing for self and in relation to others.

If we cannot care for ourselves, how can we have time to care for others?

Having fun

Life can be fulfilling and busy but where is the fun?

Needing to incorporate fun into your life is something that is as important as anything else on your journey of self-care. Some people find it easier than others, dependent on their experiences. As a responsible child and someone who took care of others, I found it particularly hard not only to think about me but to find ways to have fun. Having fun can be anything from roller skating in the park to watching a funny movie with friends. Pushing yourself out of your comfort zone, trying something new, being a child again; the freedom is unbelievable, and the list is endless. Kicking leaves in the park, rolling down hills, face painting, playing games, dancing in the living room, dancing in the street, water parks, fun fairs and all of the above can be a part of your children's life too. Children can help us to have fun, whether they are ours or someone else's. They can be a reminder of the freedom we sometimes forget we had.

What do we mean by support network?

Friends, people who treat you as an equal, who care about your wellbeing, helpful friends with good boundaries, some family members, people you trust, people who respect you, understanding people, people who accept you just the way you are, 'warts an' all', people who do not judge but accept who and how you are, all who support and accept you. Those you can be around when you are feeling happy, sad, angry, silent, bored, etc.

The next few pages are worksheets on food/alcohol/ feelings. Self-care, exercise, fun and support network. Please explore the worksheets to give you an idea of how you really take care of yourself and to see where your structure/self-esteem is to allow you time to be able to identify areas that may need to change or be improved upon. These worksheets are to support continued change; they are not for you to criticise or be negative about yourself.

WORKSHEET

Food/Feelings

Do you use food when you feel stressed? If so, which? Do you know why?

Do you use food when you feel lonely? Which?

Do you see certain foods as a treat? If so, what are they?

Do you use food when you are angry, stressed, emotional, etc? Which foods?

Do you tell yourself you need this food, etc., because you have had a stressful day?

How/When?

WORKSHEET

Alcohol/Drugs/Feelings

Do you use alcohol/drugs when you feel stressed? If so, which? Do you know why?

Do you use alcohol/drugs when you feel lonely? Which?

Do you see alcohol/drugs as a treat? If so, when?

Do you use alcohol/drugs when you are angry, stressed, emotional, etc? Which?

Do you tell yourself you need this drink/drug because you have had a stressful day?

Do you use alcohol/drugs to sleep at night?

WORKSHEET

Self-Care

What does the words self-care mean to you?

What do you do to ensure you have good self-care?

Are there areas in which your self-care needs improving?

In an ideal world, what would your self-care look like?

What are the things you like to do regarding your self-care?

WORKSHEET

Exercise

Exercise can be dancing, walking, swimming, roller skating, ice skating; anything with movement ...

What exercise do you do on a regular basis, if any?

What exercise do you enjoy?

If you were to set up an exercise routine, what would that look like?

Set a goal and start to look at what you can begin to do ...

WORKSHEET

Fun

How easy is it for you to implement fun into your life?

What ideas do you have to incorporate fun into your life?

Can you think of new ways to have fun?

How often do you have fun?

When are you going to start?

WORKSHEET

Your Support Network

What do we mean by support network?

What does your support network look like?

Do you feel you could improve on your support network?

What changes do you feel that you would like to make with the people you have in your life?

Is your support network meeting your needs?

Chapter Six

NOAH'S JOURNEY
(Male–early thirties)

Paint the night sky
While the morning waits
With a field of stars
To keep the dark at bay…

"*All you're dreaming of*" written by Liam Gallagher and Simon Aldred and was produced by Andrew Wyatt, 2020.

I am making a coffee at home listening to Liam Gallagher. Instant coffee, nonetheless. I like the taste. I am not fussy. The furthest I will go to being flamboyant is adding a splash of oat milk.

So here I am. Stood in the kitchen, mid-morning. Making a coffee, with my favourite band playing in the background.

This is normal for me. I have always liked background noise, be it music or talk radio. When I say normal, it is a new norm now. This time, I am crying my eyes out.

I am not crying because I do not like the song on the radio. I like the song. No, I love it. I am not crying because I am drinking cheap, tasteless coffee. I always have, and always will.

It is because ... I do not know why.

All I know is I feel so incredibly sad. Sad all the time. Sad to my core. The sadness is heavy, exhausting. I am not sure if it has always been there, but recently it has been showing itself. It is busting out of me, like a broken fire hydrant. I cannot keep it in. I have become prone to bursting into tears at any moment. (Fortunately, I have been alone up to now when it happens, so I must still have a measure of control over it.)

I am thirty-eight years old. Until recently, I could count on one hand how few times I have cried as a grown-up. I have never been a person who cries. Lately, though, I have cried so much it feels like my body is trying to make up for lost time. Squeezing thirty years of tears into the last month or so. It is exhausting! And I feel sad.

This was me. Summer 2020. Crying in my kitchen making coffee.

This was not the start of my sadness but the best place to begin.

To get things moving, it was another two months before I reached out to Susan for help. I am a walking cliché of a thirty-something-year-old man, working-class background, whose go-to when things were difficult or to even think about the idea of asking for help was to religiously recall the slogan 'Just get on with it/Keep calm and carry on', which seems to epitomise the culture that surrounds me. Work through it! It will be fine!

Except, this time, it was not fine. The 'carry-on' method was not working.

My partner had seen the change in me long before I thought it was evident to anyone around me. She encouraged me to speak to my friend and seek help. Eventually, I did.

Without her encouragement, I do not think I would have. It made me realise that what I was feeling was not just having an impact on me but her also; I just did not know it. I was naive in thinking I could hide or put on a brave face at what was going on (though I did not know exactly what it was that was going on, just that I needed help) and she would not notice. I did for a while, but now the cracks were in full sight. To her, at least.

I contacted Susan through a recommendation from a friend. The journey began there for me, as it took what felt like a colossal amount of time and courage to ask my friend for his help. He did not hesitate to offer help and guidance in the form of Susan's contact details.

Dare I say he was almost delighted that I asked. He was happy that I reached out. That here were these two (close-to-forty) guys chatting about mental health and not just the usual – football and work.

Day 1. Appointment with Susan. I am seeing a therapist! I was nervous, anxious, apprehensive. But also strangely calm because I had committed to the appointment. By making the appointment, I was taking the responsibility of turning up, and this was something at which I am good. Turning up. Having a task to do. Not letting people down.

Before the first call (this was winter lockdown, 2020; the appointment was via video call), although nervous, I was determined to try to not bring any preconceived ideas of what therapy looked like with me, and how this should play out.

I wanted to be as open-minded as possible and try to commit to the process as best I could. Listen and let things play out.

I was not sure it would work. Not at all. But I knew I had to give it a chance.

My expectation of myself was that I would be my normal guarded self. Have a chat and see where this may go and how it could help me. This was what I thought. I was thinking in a logical, pragmatic way. I was doing this to try and 'fix' what was wrong with me.

Something inside me had other ideas.

From my recollection, almost immediately after Susan and I introduced ourselves, the first question came ... 'How are you?' That was it. I burst into tears, broke down right there.

My emotions were not going to let me poker face this one. My normal socially stoic self was not abiding by any social norms.

I was talking to a total stranger. A cavalcade of tears flowing swiftly followed with the compulsory 'I'm sorry, I'm sorry ... I don't normally do this.'

I could feel my body crumbling in front of this person, and I could not hold it back. My guess is something in me knew this was a safe space to release. Like a pressure cooker, I had managed to keep it in for so long, but now was the release.

The rest of the session is a little blurred to me now. All I remember is having this feeling throughout my body of relief. My shoulders felt lighter than they had for a long time. Like I had a mental massage, and all the muscle and joint pain in my head had released momentarily.

This felt like a change. Even after one session, I felt more positive. I had a conversation about me and did not feel too embarrassed. It felt strangely comfortable, despite the tears.

Over the forthcoming months, Susan and I began to dig a little deeper. I started to open up about my story, starting with the present: Where am I now? What am I doing in work, socially, for self? How do I feel?

We began to understand a fundamental lack of self-esteem. This was just the beginning of important realisations I had on my journey, and not one I would have come to understand without Susan's help.

This was not an easy thing to understand. Learning and realising that I have no self-worth and the critical voice inside is not helping me was an upsetting thing to come to understand. It has been normal for as long as I can remember.

Through this understanding, we began to produce simple but significant changes to my daily habits, such as making conscious efforts to get more sleep, eat three meals a day and exercise.

It is hard to explain and do justice to the impact these changes had on my mental health and self-esteem, but they had such an amazing impact.

I have remained consistent with these changes; they have become habitual.

The way Susan encouraged and helped me implement these additions to my daily life has helped to make them stick. It is because I am doing them for me. And that is OK! It is not just OK; it is the best reason to do these things.

There was no judgement, no 'You should be doing this!' It was through understanding my situation and the way in which she implemented certain strategies that felt natural, or as comfortable as it could have been.

As these changes started to take hold and have a positive impact on my self-esteem, we began to explore my story.

My father left the family when I was young, around ten years old. I thought this did not really have an impact on me. I did not like my father very much; he was not a good man. But I knew myself, on reflection (prior to therapy), that I had tried to please, impress, garner his attention as a child, but it was never forthcoming.

I think my dad leaving always felt like it would be an easy out, even when I was young. I would not talk about it to anyone. I simply became an angry teenager who refused to show 'weakness', which in turn often meant I showed no emotion. Always feeling alone, not allowing myself to trust people, despite being from a large family. (On my mother's side, I had five uncles and aunts.)

I still struggle with this feeling today. Being alone even when in a group.

As I got older, I would fight the idea of being a failure, or the voice in my head would punish me if things did not work out perfectly because I did not want to be that cliché. The kid whose dad left so he could fail through life and use it as an excuse.

This way of thinking did not help.

We (Susan and I) discussed this and the wider impact my upbringing may have had on my feelings about myself and learnt behaviours. That the punitive internal dialogue was much more complex than my father leaving. It was a combination of factors much wider than I had thought, that I did not understand or was simply not aware of until talking about it in therapy.

The therapy was personal and tailored, which has made it feel highly effective. We not only talk but there are visual exercises. These helped me. As a visual thinker, these activities had a visceral impact and helped me understand myself better.

Over time, it became apparent that these exercises and the talking was the first time in my life where I had taken time to think about myself. Slowing down and starting to really take care of myself. And doing so without feeling guilty that I should be working, doing something 'more productive'.

I have made positive progress since seeking out Susan and beginning my journey in therapy. It is not something I measure, like I would have done in work, but I am measuring my progress based on how I feel, and that self-awareness is the biggest step I could have hoped to make on this journey, though I did not know it at the time.

I still have difficult days. Days when it feels like the world is closing in all around, in a thick, blinding fog. Or I just want to cry and am overcome with emotion. (I still find myself triggered by certain songs.) The difference now is I feel much more equipped to recognise these feelings and react positively to them.

I can acknowledge how I feel and in doing so acknowledge that feeling like this is okay. I feel better prepared to not sink as far into the fog, and when I do find myself there, I have tools that I can use to climb out.

One day, in the future, I will be singing that Liam Gallagher song aloud in my kitchen with a big smile on my face. Though I cannot promise the quality of the coffee will improve, but do you know what, I am okay with that.

Working alliance

Noah initially came to see me as he had experienced the loss of his grandmothers, as well as his recent job, and felt that life was stressful. He stated he was in a good relationship but had concerns regarding his worth, anxiety and general stress.

Noah acknowledged the importance of coming to therapy to explore his feelings, and as this was his first time in therapy, he also acknowledged to himself that sharing his emotions was part of the process he needed.

He began to share his experience – he was the middle child; an older brother and a younger sister. His father left the family unit when he was a young boy, and although he did not initially acknowledge the impact of this on him, he later realised that this had played a part in his thoughts about himself and certain behaviours.

Noah talked about his loneliness and lack of nurturing as a child, not due to intentional harm but due to the consequences of his mother needing to work and manage as a single parent. He used the space to explore his feelings of responsibility, not being good enough, the violence of his father and trying to find his authentic self.

Noah slowly began to recognise patterns in his behaviour that kept him stuck, although stating they had been a useful distraction previously. They were now detrimental to his wellbeing. The grief that the client had experienced appeared to have opened a series of thoughts; who he is and why he behaves in certain ways. He explored his internal critical dialogue, his high expectations of self, his loss of childhood, which all appeared to come to the surface at once. Noah took every step at a considered pace, which allowed him to reflect and process his journey. We explored breathing techniques and mindfulness for his anxiety, and various other techniques building his self-esteem, assertion skills, the use of boundaries and intimacy within his relationship and challenging his negative internal dialogue. After a period, he began to explore things he enjoyed, like cooking, playing football, growing plants, gardening, painting. He then built a routine that he could follow to support continued change. He started to grow in esteem, stating he had more value for self and recognised the importance of taking time for self. While working with this client, I acknowledged the importance of slowing things down, talking in pictures as it helped his process as an artist. Finding various creative ways of working, recognising and encouraging his gift as an artist also supported his growth in esteem. I valued each step on his journey and was respectful of the pace. I was pleased that he felt able to take the time he needed for himself, valuing his input, respecting his knowledge and appreciating his openness and trust in the process. He is an intelligent, talented, kind man with the potential to achieve his goals in life, taking the time and space to do so without rushing.

Chapter Seven

BOUNDARIES AND SELF-ESTEEM

As children, if we experience mistreatment or abuse, our child within tends to go into hiding, often deep within the unconscious part of self. As the child recovers/heals, they decide that they do not need to hide as much and begin building trust in safe relationships.

What do we mean by boundaries?

Boundaries are set by us to protect us. They are our limits as to what we are willing to accept and what we are not. Without an awareness of healthy boundaries, it would be difficult to ascertain who it is safe to be around. Without boundaries, we may not feel we have a self. And without boundaries, we cannot have a healthy self-esteem.

In our daily life experience, we have many opportunities for growth. That growth includes the physical, mental, emotional and spiritual realms of our awareness, experience and consciousness. Awareness of our boundaries helps us in that growth.

A healthy boundary is not a wall. A healthy boundary provides us with our healthy human needs, which may include time/space where we can be alone and away from others, including noise distractions.

Healthy boundaries:
- Protect us
- Are non-invasive
- Are present and clear
- Allow other people in when desirable and appropriate
- Are assertive, not aggressive
- Are appropriate
- Are protective
- Are firm
- Are flexible
- Are receptive
- Are not set by others
- Are not hurtful, harmful or manipulative

We learn from our parents/caregivers what are healthy/unhealthy boundaries.

Without an awareness of healthy boundaries, it can be difficult for us to sort out who it is unsafe to be around, which may include people who are toxic for us and even some people who may mistreat or abuse us. Without boundaries, it would be hard to define oneself and know oneself, and without boundaries, we cannot have a healthy self. So, by being aware of and having healthy boundaries, we can define ourselves, know oneself and have healthy self-esteem.

The key to good boundaries is knowing our inner life. This includes our beliefs, thoughts, feelings, decisions, choices and experiences. It also includes our wants, needs, sensations within our body, intuitions and even unconscious factors of our life. If we are aware of or out of touch with our inner life, we cannot know all our boundary limits. When we are aware of our inner life, we can more readily know our boundaries.

Working through conflict – What is mine and what is not mine?

Present – The conflict in the here and now. The meaning of our differences may vary in the actual dynamics of the conflict. It is about working through the levels to arrive at a resolution. Knowing oneself and one's boundaries will enable this to occur. For example: being honest about being wrong or getting it wrong. Being aware of here-and-now dynamics and the processes we go through. What we bring to the relationship and how we feel as well as acknowledging difference and not expecting someone else to feel or act the same as us. Checking out our feelings and thoughts, separating them from the other person while exploring the here and now rather than staying stuck in any kind of projection or expectation.

Past – The unconscious part of ourselves of which we are unaware. At this level, our feelings are often intense and overwhelming. Common sense resolution escapes us. To help us become more aware of this kind of unfinished business, we might ask ourselves the following question: 'Of whom or what from my past does, or might, this conflict remind me?'

With whom was the conflict?

When was it?

How old was I?

What happened?

What happened next?

Did I ever try to resolve it? If so, how?

My internalised messages or beliefs - This includes painful material, patterns or messages that we may have repressed into our unconscious mind which we may still believe about ourselves (playing old tapes repeatedly). To help us be more aware of unfinished business, we might ask ourselves the following questions:

- What rigid rules or negative messages did I hear or learn around past conflict?
- What beliefs, belief systems or attitudes did I form around past conflict?
- What aspect or part of the person/s in this past conflict might I have incorporated or taken in as though it was now a part of myself?

It is our child within/true self who does the work in resolving conflicts and working through this kind of projection, which can also be deemed as transference. It is our false self or negative ego that contributes to the formation of conflict. However, that false self or ego may also be a 'friend in disguise' at times, as it might be trying to tell us something important or help us survive what feels like an overwhelming or dangerous situation. While there are no fixed rules about recognising these kinds of boundary invasions that we call projections, this does not mean that every time any of these occur, it automatically indicates the presence of an unconscious defence of projection.

Even though we may advance as we form healthier boundaries, conflicts related to projection do not go away. Like the ducks in a carnival shooting gallery, unconscious material tends to keep manifesting itself in our lives. The difference is, as we advance, these conflicts tend to slow down, and our ability to be aware allows us to work through them. We become more able to identify and work through projections, transferences and conflict more easily and rapidly, as we bring our unconscious material more fully into our conscious awareness. As a result, we form more fulfilling, close, intimate relationships.

Mental and emotional areas of our life

Beliefs, ideas, feelings, decisions and choices.

For example, when told what you 'should' believe, think, feel decide or choose. So that your boundaries may be adhered to at that time.

Has anyone ever accused you of or blamed you for something you did not do?

If yes, how did you feel? Are you still tolerating this behaviour?

If so, you do not have to. This pain, confusion or attempts at control or manipulation may be theirs, not yours. With awareness of your inner life, clear boundaries/limits, you can handle or at times prevent such a boundary invasion, thus avoiding unnecessary pain and suffering.

Other mental and emotional areas where personal boundaries are important include our energy, sexuality, needs, time alone, intuitions and even our individual differences.

Do you feel anyone has ever drained your energy so much that you have neglected your own needs?

Possibility: You may have experienced a lack of awareness of your inner life, including your needs. You may have been people pleasing to the detriment of yourself (active co-dependence). This is a set-up of boundary violation whereby more unnecessary pain and suffering may occur.

Some other mental and emotional areas where personal boundaries are helpful include love, interests, relationships, participation, roles and rules.

A principle we can use is to keep our boundaries as flexible as feels appropriate for us. For our wants and needs and other aspects of our inner life. Setting a healthy boundary or withdrawing if we wish. This is another example of using our boundaries in a healthy way.

Reflect on the above and see if there are any changes you would like to make, or see if you feel whether you want to set some new boundaries. You could, for instance, start afresh and talk to those people closest to you about your new boundaries and ways of being.

Healthy boundaries and limits

As I heal my child within, I realise my true self and begin to live from and as I really am. Discovering healthy boundaries and limits is not just how useful they are to us but allows us to progressively increase our awareness that healthy boundaries protect our wellbeing and integrity of our true self. As we heal, we learn that healthy boundaries and limits are necessary in several critical areas of our lives.

Knowing our boundaries and limits are healthy:

To sense the usefulness or non-usefulness of a boundary – a boundary must be present in our awareness to some degree. If it is not, then we may not be able to set it or choose to let it go.

Appropriate – based on our inner life. The boundaries are set to include our beliefs, thoughts, feelings, decisions, choices, wants, needs, intuitions and more. So, knowing what is coming up for us in our life is crucial in setting healthy boundaries and having healthy relationships.

Protective – This boundary is useful to help protect the wellbeing and integrity of our child within.

Clarity – To be clear about the boundary set for us and others with whom we are setting the boundary limit.

Firmness – To get what we want or need. How firm do we want to set the boundary or limit for a period, to get what we want or need? Or to relax the boundary limit to get what we want or need?

Maintenance – Do we need to maintain or hold firm a specific boundary or limit or to relax that boundary?

Flexibility – To have healthy relationships, we need to let go of boundaries and limits when appropriate.

Receptive – Would it be useful to loosen the boundary to let another person, place, thing, behaviour or experience in?

Modern psychology theory and practice now clearly differentiates between the self, which is the true self, and the ego as being two separate but related parts of our psyche. The true self being the consciousness and essence that we really are, the ego or false self is our assistant who helps us deal with the world. The true self as being separate from the false self or ego, it is now accurate to think of a boundary as being a creative dynamic of the true self or self since the true self makes and uses healthy boundaries to protect and maintain its integrity and wellbeing. The ego can/does, however, make unhealthy boundaries as walls of separation between us and other people, places and things. It may even distort or blur our attempts at forming healthy relationships.

Thinking about your ego in terms of self-esteem and boundaries, can you see or are you aware of any repetitive patterns in your life?

How has the above impacted on your boundaries?

How has the above impacted on your self-esteem?

What, if anything, has changed about your understanding over time?

Take a moment to explore the above at length and use a piece of scrap paper to write notes or journalise your experiences.

WORKSHEET

What are your boundaries?

Think about your own personal boundaries and write them down.

Where did they come from?

Are you happy with the boundaries you have?

How have your boundaries, or lack of, impacted on your self-esteem?

Do you think you need to change your boundaries? If so, why?

What, if anything, would you change?

WORKSHEET

Circle the answers that apply to you.

I can make up my own mind.
Never   Seldom   Occasionally   Often   Usually

I have difficulty saying no.
Never   Seldom   Occasionally   Often   Usually

I feel as if my happiness depends on other people.
Never   Seldom   Occasionally   Often   Usually

It is hard for me to look a person in the eye.
Never   Seldom   Occasionally   Often   Usually

I find myself getting involved with people who end up hurting me.
Never   Seldom   Occasionally   Often   Usually

I trust others.
Never   Seldom   Occasionally   Often   Usually

I would rather attend to others than attend to myself.
Never   Seldom   Occasionally   Often   Usually

Other people's opinions are more important than mine.
Never   Seldom   Occasionally   Often   Usually

I have difficulty asking for what I want or what I need.
Never   Seldom   Occasionally   Often   Usually

I feel anxious, scared or afraid.
Never   Seldom   Occasionally   Often   Usually

I spend my time and energy helping others so much that I neglect my own
wants and needs.
Never   Seldom   Occasionally   Often   Usually

It is hard for me to know what I believe and think.
Never   Seldom   Occasionally   Often   Usually

I feel as if my happiness depends on circumstances outside of me.
Never   Seldom   Occasionally   Often   Usually

I have a tough time knowing what I really feel.
Never   Seldom   Occasionally   Often   Usually

It is hard for me to make decisions.
Never   Seldom   Occasionally   Often   Usually

I feel angry.
Never   Seldom   Occasionally   Often   Usually

I do not get much time to spend alone.
Never   Seldom   Occasionally   Often   Usually

I tend to take on the moods of people close to me.
Never   Seldom   Occasionally   Often   Usually

I feel overly sensitive to criticism.
Never   Seldom   Occasionally   Often   Usually

I feel hurt.
Never   Seldom   Occasionally   Often   Usually

People take or use my things without asking me.
Never   Seldom   Occasionally   Often   Usually

I would rather go along with another person or other people than express what I would really like to do.
Never   Seldom   Occasionally   Often   Usually

Some people I lend things to never give them back.
Never   Seldom   Occasionally   Often   Usually

I tend to stay in relationships that are hurting me.
Never   Seldom   Occasionally   Often   Usually

I feel an emptiness, as though something is missing in my life.
Never   Seldom   Occasionally   Often   Usually

I tend to get caught up in the middle of other people's problems.
Never   Seldom   Occasionally   Often   Usually

When someone I am with acts up in public, I tend to be embarrassed.
Never   Seldom   Occasionally   Often   Usually

I feel sad.
Never   Seldom   Occasionally   Often   Usually

I prefer to rely on what others say about what I should believe and do about religious or spiritual matters.

Never   Seldom   Occasionally   Often   Usually

I tend to take on or feel what others are feeling.

Never   Seldom   Occasionally   Often   Usually

I put more into relationships than I get out of them.

Never   Seldom   Occasionally   Often   Usually

I feel responsible for other people's feelings.

Never   Seldom   Occasionally   Often   Usually

My friends and acquaintances have a tough time keeping secrets or confidences that I tell them.

Never   Seldom   Occasionally   Often   Usually

Once you have completed the above, take some time to reflect on your answers and whether you feel you need to make any changes to your boundaries. Also, it might be a suitable time to review your assertiveness and self-esteem.

Chapter Eight

LILLY'S JOURNEY
(Lilly–female, twenties)

Lilly came to see me to discuss her relationship break-up, how she felt and the impact the relationship had on her self-esteem/confidence. During the time we worked together, she informed me that the young man she had been seeing would make negative comments towards her and had been quite controlling in his behaviour, but due to his history of substance use and mental health, she tolerated these behaviours. Further exploration led to her identifying psychological abuse and coercive control. Once she began to acknowledge how the behaviour had impacted on her as well as her value of self/confidence and increased anxiety, she came to realise that she had been right to explore this, and she was not imagining things or being difficult, as was suggested by her ex-boyfriend.

Client history – Lilly is one of two children, both parents still married, no real expectations of her or pressure to achieve, and she regarded her upbringing as quite stable. She stated that she had been encouraged by family members to settle down at some stage and have a family of her own, which was the only expectation; however, she wanted more for her life and wanted to achieve a good career, have her own money and be independent. She did not feel supported by her family to achieve this, nor was she encouraged to travel or venture out into the world due to this not being expected from her family of origin. She felt quite stifled by the family and stated that they were not people who she felt able to talk to about her feelings or experiences, and that she had been previously deemed overly sensitive when she tried to express her feelings. She stated that she found it hard to communicate with her family about her career and future goals as she felt it was seen as her expecting too much or that she should be satisfied to lead a more traditional life.

Quite early in her career, the client began to travel with her work and felt happy with her career. This was an area of her life where she felt confident and competent; however, when she became involved in a relationship, her career and life changed, whereby she became, as she describes it, different, not herself. Doing what her partner wanted her to do, being how he wanted her to be and questioning herself as well as her actions.

She is a successful young woman who is very capable, intelligent and self-aware. She is compassionate, considerate and tolerant of what was perceived as disrespectful behaviour. As our relationship built, she was able to see that there had been previous patterns in past relationships. Not to the same extent but certainly previous unhelpful comments and put-downs. We began to work on her understanding of repetitive patterns and how to change these patterns and began building her value of worth.

She presented as all of the above and more. I was impressed by her ability to see herself and by the compassion she showed others. I was concerned with the lack of compassion she showed herself and her vulnerability to abuse. We went on a journey to explore her lack of value of self and what actions she could take to build her self-esteem.

Once Lilly had identified patterns in her behaviour and the impact this had on her life/relationships, she made the decision to change. She soon began to implement changes that would work for her. Once she acknowledged that she had choices, which is something she appeared unaware of initially, she then decided to challenge some of her decision-making regarding her relationships with men, explore her options, set goals for her future, practise her assertion skills and build her self-worth.

Lilly completed worksheets on the subject and while going through her learning, she decided to end the relationship with the young man she initially talked about. During her time working through and building her esteem, she moved away with work and although she continued for a brief time to have online therapy, she came to a point whereby she felt she had enough tools to lead a healthy, happy life.

Experience as written by Lilly

When I first found Susan, I was not entirely sure why I was entering therapy. I just knew that what I was experiencing was not your average heartbreak, and there had been a fundamental change in how I saw myself and how I behaved that troubled me. Susan was patient with me and provided a safe and welcoming space for me to work out my own experience, without using labelling words like emotional abuse, which was what I had experienced, among other things. If a word or label as such was used straight off the bat, I would not have been able to comprehend or identify with it, but going through this journey with Susan allowed me to accept this and in turn heal from the experience.

I had always considered myself a confident and self-assured woman with high self-awareness, so unknowingly being in an abusive relationship was not something that I or my close friends or family could see happening throughout that time. With Susan, I learnt that confidence and self-esteem are two quite different things, and that relationship was one part of the story, something tangible that happened, but throughout therapy I was able to understand how I had come to be in that situation and how I had allowed, accepted and sometimes even welcomed it.

It is not an understatement to say that my short time in therapy with Susan has equipped me with tools that I will carry with me for the rest of my life, while also piquing my curiosity on more systemic issues, like how women often find themselves in similar situations and what, as a society, needs to change to prevent more women and girls falling into this heartbreaking cycle.

Chapter Nine

RELATIONSHIPS AND SELF-ESTEEM

We tend to believe that people see us as we see ourselves. Low self-esteem can cause self-doubt. The internal dialogue may be: Will people like me? Will my friends/partner continue to love and support me?

When people have low self-esteem, they can easily experience bullying or manipulation by others. This can lead to excessive dependence on another person. Also, low self-esteem can cause jealously, which can be toxic for the relationship. Signs of low self-esteem in a relationship can be anxiety, inability to communicate, jealousy, lack of honesty, self-criticism, fear, negative image, etc.

Low self-esteem can become tiring to others, who may see the person as unable to help themselves. This can become a lack of mutual respect, which can cause the relationship to suffer. Also, the person with low self-esteem can sometimes have what can be perceived as a victim mentality, blaming others for their problems and failing to take responsibility for their actions. They can attract negative people into their lives or controlling people who want to manipulate them. Being in victim mode or mentality can be a defence behaviour which was learnt to protect self from abuse and as a tool for survival. As someone who was stuck in victim mode for many years, I have learnt it is really about understanding self as well as being aware of how to enable movement from this position.

Before beginning any relationship, I feel it is important to be open about expectations, needs and wants. Describing the relationship you want and the qualities you are looking for in that other person and what you feel you have to offer. We can sometimes have experience of being caught up in the attraction of that other person rather than the importance of what they have to offer the relationship.

While boundaries and limits can sometimes be an 'issue', it is helpful to describe them more accurately as being a basic dynamic in relation to person to person, place, behaviour or experience. Setting healthy boundaries and limits at any time, anywhere or letting go of them whenever you choose.

Low self-esteem can lead to a high tolerance of inappropriate behaviour – this may keep you from leaving an unhealthy relationship. It may loosen the boundaries even more, to such an extent that you do experience mistreatment. Allowing others to mistreat you, so you will not leave. With already low self-esteem, it may not dawn on you that you do not deserve to be treated in this way.

There are times in our lives and in our relationships when we might feel our self-esteem is becoming eroded. It is important to acknowledge how we communicate.

Do you often criticise your partner?

Is this something you have learnt to do?

Take a look at your family dynamics. Are you repeating patterns of behaviour that you have learnt/experienced?

What messages are you sending your partner, and how do they feel about these messages?

How are you communicating with each other?

When we criticise each other, we are not being accepting. The truth is, we are all flawed. None of us is perfect, but we are human.

Is the seat not being put down on the toilet really the issue? Or is there something else going on?

In my experience of past relationships, it has been about my own unhappiness when I have criticised partners. How I was feeling about myself and my own self-esteem was little to do with them. I believe that when we are unhappy, we show that by how we communicate with others. Unhappiness spreads unhappiness. Once we value ourselves, we tend to then choose or attract the right relationship/partner. I have had enough unhealthy relationships to know when something is healthy and thankfully worked hard to change patterns of behaviour from my past to ensure that I am aware to ensure I take responsibility for me as well as my actions.

Taking a look at your family dynamics and what you may feel you have brought to your present relationships ... Take a moment to see how history can repeat itself and what you may feel needs to change ...

Did your parents get along?

Did they express love for one another?

Did they talk about their feelings?

Did they encourage you to talk about your feelings?

Were there lots of arguments, fighting, criticisms?

Did they avoid feelings and go silent instead?

Did you hear them praise and appreciate each other (working as a team)?

What do you think you learnt from your parents, caregivers, adults around you about relationships?

We are often not conscious of how our self-esteem impacts on our relationships and how we get our self-esteem from these relationships. We can expect our partners to grow our worth by praising us, telling us we look good, etc., but if we do not feel that ourselves then it is a false sense of esteem. We can also use our lack of worth to try to gain power over our partner and put them down in situations where we feel more capable, etc.

If a partner has low self-esteem, we may feel we need to give them value and praise to know their worth. This is not necessarily a terrible thing as we all need acknowledgement and praise at some point in our lives; however, it is equally important, if not more important, for us to be able to praise and affirm ourselves. It is not about giving yourself a tough time if you feel that your relationship is not what you had hoped, or after being more aware of your self-esteem, you realise it is not what you want. The whole learning is about you, not anyone else. It is about awareness first and change second. Look at it like an exercise in getting to know yourself, your wants, needs and aspirations.

WORKSHEET

Give yourself time to think about when you gave praise to your partner/yourself. What did you say and how did you say it?

How often do you tell yourself or your partner what an excellent job they have done or how proud you are of you/them?

What would you like to say to yourself/partner about how you/they are as a person and what qualities you/they have as people?

How did you learn about relationships?

What were your parents/caregivers like in their relationship?

Did you come from a loving environment?

What does a healthy relationship look like to you?

Family dynamics/repeating what you learnt –

WORKSHEET

What words to do you continue to repeat to your children that you were told?

What do you feel you have gained from your experiences that you can now share with your children?

Do you feel that you are doing things differently/better?

If so, what is different/better?

How would you like your children to remember their experiences? Telling their story ...

Assertiveness in relationships and the impact on esteem

Assertion provides an important source of self-esteem as both promote the practice of behaving as if an individual. Assertiveness is strongly associated with increased self-esteem. Self-esteem problems express themselves invariably in terms of either passivity or aggression. Assertiveness techniques help us to protect our own rights and feelings and help us to take a problem-solving approach rather than an accepting, bitter or complaining approach to life's challenges.

It is important to explore certain roadblocks to assertiveness and myths that encourage non-assertive behaviour.

See below and begin to identify those that may be true for you.

Roadblocks:

1 If I assert myself in any relationship, others will get angry at me.
2 If I do assert myself and others do become angry with me, it will be awful; I will be devastated.
3 Although I prefer others to be straightforward with me, I am afraid that if I am open with them and say 'No', I will hurt their feelings.
4 If my assertion hurts others, I then become responsible for their feelings.
5 It is wrong to turn down legitimate requests as others may think I am selfish and will then not like me.
6 I must avoid making statements or asking questions that might make me look ignorant or stupid.
7 Assertive people are cold and uncaring. If I am assertive, I will be so unpleasant, which means others will not like me.

Assertive counterparts

1 If I assert myself, the results may be positive, negative or neutral. However, since assertion involves legitimate rights, the odds of having positive results are in my favour.
2 Even if others become angry, I can handle it without falling apart. If I assert myself when it is appropriate, I do not have to feel responsible for the feelings of others.
3 If I am assertive, others may or may not feel hurt as others are not necessarily more fragile than I am.

4 Even if others experience hurt by my assertive behaviour, I can let them know that my intention is not to cause harm. Although, at times, they may struggle due to my assertive behaviour, it is important I do not deem them to be so fragile but respect differences.

5 Even legitimate requests can be refused, sometimes; it is acceptable to consider my needs before others. I cannot always please others.

6 It is okay to lack information or make a mistake; it just shows that I am human.

7 Assertive people can be direct and honest and behave appropriately. They show a genuine concern for other people's rights and feelings as well as their own. Their assertiveness enriches their relationships with others.

Being assertive for me is about immediacy, being able to say my truth in that moment even if others disagree or have another opinion. Valuing yourself enough to have a voice and coming from a good intention, not a harmful one. No put-downs of others, just expressing your opinion in an appropriate manner by allowing yourself value and a voice. Being immediate, it not only takes the power out of things but stops resentment building and things becoming ugly as well as out of control. Being mindful how we speak to each other, coming from the 'I', not the 'you', talking about how you feel in the situation, not blaming the other person for your feelings, etc.

For example, If someone has an opinion that you disagree with and you do not state your view, only acknowledging their view and opinion. If you did do this, you may feel that the other person is the only one to have a voice, which can secretly build resentments. This can lead to angry feelings and frustrations, which can later come out over something simple, like them spilling a cup of coffee and you then becoming angry over this issue. When we build resentments, this can impact on our self-esteem and our value of others.

When I talk about immediacy, I do not mean you need to say aloud what you are thinking but that giving yourself permission is important as this allows your self-esteem to grow. For instance, not allowing others to push their opinions on you if you disagree, or if you have something to say about a subject, say it, or if you feel something is important to you, state it. Allow yourself the time and patience to be and feel how you are in that moment. This all takes time and practice, and I would initially encourage you to practise with people you know well and who are closest to you, then slowly develop your skills of assertion around strangers, work colleagues, etc.

Being assertive is not being aggressive; it is not about raising your voice or shouting to get heard. It is allowing yourself a voice, an opinion pushing through the anxiety/fear and believing that you are worth it.

It has taken me years to become the person I am today and a lot of practice as well as many mistakes along the way. I have learnt to assert myself in areas that I need to and to let things go in areas that I do not need to.

When being assertive, I maintain a calm manner and tone of voice as that is my natural state. Assertiveness for me is about stating my truth, giving or having a valid opinion and allowing myself a voice. Keeping it simple, so that others are aware of my view, as well as stating facts and not letting or allowing others to intimidate or force their views upon me. Agreeing to have a difference of opinion too.

There have been many times in my life when I have not said how I have felt or not allowed myself the time or a voice, which has led to consequences of being a victim in certain situations, past abuse and intimidation from colleagues as well as management in various areas of my previous work. I have learnt in some ways the hard way but am glad that I am able to assert myself today. If I can overcome some of the areas in my life, then I believe that others can too.

Thinking of the above, and when you have completed the exercise, have a look at the worksheet overleaf and see what changes you would like to make.

WORKSHEET

Can you be assertive?

If not, what happens?

If yes, how are you assertive?

Do you feel that your assertion skills need improvement? If so, how?

How would you like to be assertive and in what areas of your life do you feel you need to be?

How can you begin to practise your assertion skills and where would you like to start?

I plan to ...

Chapter Ten

ANNA'S JOURNEY
(Anna–female, thirties)

When you think about yourself, what does your value mean to you?

Hearing those words immediately made me shudder and my body abruptly answered for me. There was no way of stopping it. My neck tightened, becoming rigid, and my jaw locked as though I was in pain. Hearing the word 'value' being related to me made me feel a lot more than I was aware. My body recoiled inside, and my deep sadness showed.

As a small girl, I was always the happy-go-lucky, colourful little girl that would put smiles on people's faces. Full of life, singing, tap dancing and putting on shows for people. The little performer, who was a consistent and positive dose of sunshine for people. Always kind, looking after others and working hard, touching people's hearts. I wanted to make others proud, which came natural to me. I had been gifted with the intention to work hard towards an exciting future to be thankful for.

Each day, growing up was packed with a great deal of tutoring and after-school sporting and musical events. I was an A-class student with a scholarship who was deeply scared, anxious and overwrought. Leading up to school exams, my brain and body felt as though they were shutting off. The stern narrator inside my head, jabbing and probing at me, telling me 'I should' be better than this, was a constant voice that was getting louder, shouting to go faster.

This continued throughout my working life for the next decade until one day I woke up in hospital. My body this time had succeeded in shutting down. I was on my way to play tennis and I fell in the middle of the road, unconscious. Everything all went silent for the next seven days.

This event nearly took my life. I knew I needed to understand how to wake up to myself and to the agony I was putting myself under. The narrator in my head was cruel. Harmful. I would never dream or want to speak to anyone in the way I spoke to myself. At work, I was on the brink of burning myself out. I was feeding this painful voice like an addict, working ridiculously long hours, putting everything and anyone else before looking after myself. There was truly little value left for me.

My relationship, which had become emotionally abusive, had ended while in lockdown. It was a huge relief getting my freedom back. I knew this was the time of survival, to face myself for the last time. To find myself and like me as my person before anything or anyone else. I was thirty-five years old and realised that if I did not start standing up for myself now, I was never going to be able to, for the life I was truly hoping for myself. I felt so much shame that I had felt broken or had allowed myself to be a victim. I knew I needed to work out how to connect back to the actual me within, to find me now and pull her out to look after her.

Susan enabled me to take off all the different labels I was carrying, to allow myself the space to become kinder and gentler to myself. Giving myself permission of this time, I was able to start understanding the relationship I had with myself, to connect with my love, calmly and considerately. This was the first time I was truly putting myself first and realising the importance of gaining my own worth for myself. I have learnt several types of tools on how to protect my value, which I now cherish, and have learnt how to manage my inner narration. This is my gift to myself, and I have learnt how to protect it. This journey has been life-changing in developing my self-esteem, enabling me to hear and listen to myself, to be able to trust the person I am. A person that I love and am proud of, with a voice that is kind, forgiving and gentle. It is also strong and dependent enough to put down my barriers to protect myself from myself, habits and from others. I will not allow myself to give away easily to others my hard-earned value that brings me sunshine. This is me and who I am. I feel incredibly lucky and thankful that I belong to me to prioritise. I look forward to the next chapter of my journey and more happy endings to come.

Working alliance

When I first started working with Anna, she presented as a happy-go-lucky kind of woman with a very cheerful disposition, which I was immediately drawn to. I liked her energy and zest for life but also noted a performance within that. When working with Anna for a while, we explored her self-image, her need for acceptance and the lack of value she had of herself, often being taken advantage of, especially within the workplace.

Anna was keen to explore change and often worked hard to achieve it; however, there were many attempts that often led Anna to find herself returning to old patterns of behaviour that were harmful. We explored this at length, her need for acceptance as well as the masks she got used to wearing and the labels she continued to wear.

Anna had experienced burnout, and I was genuinely concerned about her wellbeing. We tried all sorts of ways to implement tools; some that would work for a while and some that just did not work at all. Whatever the presenting issue, Anna was always there to accept the challenge and try her best.

We agreed that Anna's trying was the issue, and therefore less trying and more mindfulness and nurturing would be the action. Anna began to practise a healthier, improved way of being, increasing her self-care, time for self, tea breaks, meditation breaks, etc.

Anna saw the benefits and in turn this allowed her harsh internal critic to reduce. She began to take time for herself, recognising patterns in her behaviour that were unhelpful and giving herself the patience as well as love she yearned for from others.

Anna is naturally a positive being and she really started to shine through but in a more authentic way. This was not her specific goal; she was just trying to be herself without the harsh internal critic driving her.

We came to a place within her therapy whereby she felt ready to check in now and then, eventually practising with the tools she had gained without the support.

Getting to know Anna and her experiences was for me an important learning, both therapeutically and personally, as someone like Anna, who is so experienced at hiding her pain, could easily have gotten missed. Anna is and continues to be an amazingly strong, positive, considerate, kind woman, who is now able to use that kindness and consideration towards herself. I recognised her light within, which she continues to shine brightly.

Chapter Eleven

THE LABELS WE WEAR, THE ROLES WE PLAY AND THE IMPACT ON OUR SELF-ESTEEM

The labels we wear

The labels we wear, or should I say the labels we are given, have a significant impact on our value of self. Having had many labels growing up, no doubt coupled with the environment in which I was born, I was left feeling worthless, ashamed, anxious and sometimes afraid. Some of the labels were from my own family members and were perceived at that time as just teasing or a source of fun. I was often told I was oversensitive, and I would cry when I felt hurt by comments made that had an impact on my value of worth/self-esteem.

Labels are often what we are given and then repeat to ourselves over time, keeping that internal critic going, keeping us in the same place where some may say we are comfortable, but really I believe it is only common to us, not comfortable; we just tell ourselves that to make sense of it all and that is why we remain in it.

The names and labels I was given and how I was perceived by others over time informed beliefs within myself. I do not feel any of these things today, and I understand why people said what they said, often coming from a place of low self-worth too. It is, however, hard now to repeat them, having experienced the impact on my younger self. I feel compassion and love for her today, which has allowed me to let go of the old hurts I once felt. I know who I am today, and I am none of those labels as each has left me over time, leaving my true self behind. I can even laugh at some of them today, but it just goes to show, when you are younger and more vulnerable, how they can hurt so much.

My labels and their impact meant that I did not value myself. I thought I was worthless; no one would love me, and I was damaged. For years, I felt unattractive, worthless and less in comparison to others, which impacted on many areas of my life, including my weight, which fluctuated for many years. I could not get a healthy relationship with food but when I gained an understanding of the harm I was causing to myself and the knowledge that I could change everything, I did. I now enjoy cooking, making meals, enjoying the process of taking care of me, sometimes others, as well as having others cook for me. Whenever I am criticised for being … or about my appearance or however I appear to others, 'I am me', I am happy with my me and do my best to take care of this precious body I have. Challenging the negative thoughts daily allowed me to replace them with more positive, useful thoughts which I still practise today. The voice inside my head that used to tell me I was worthless now says 'You are a kind, considerate, loving human being and I love you very much.'

WORKSHEET

What labels do you still wear?

What labels, if any, have you let go of?

What labels do you feel you want to let go of, and which do you struggle to let go of?

Do you know who you are without the labels?

Are you fearful of letting go of these labels, and if so, what are your fears?

What plan would you put in place that would work for you to start removing these old labels ...?

Making changes

Using certain techniques that fit for you, you can begin the process of not criticising yourself. Think about what you have learnt so far and begin to put these things into practice on your worksheet overleaf. Think of ways that will work for you, including affirmations, being creative, challenging negative thoughts, separating fantasy from reality, etc.

WORKSHEET

How are you going to begin the practice of not criticising yourself?

How are you going to begin to look at your positive characteristics?

What is your plan to be gentle, kind and patient with self?

How will you start the process of acknowledging that no one is perfect but human?

How will you begin to reinforce what you need to know, not resisting the importance of changing?

How will you begin to stop the punishment, blame, guilt and shame?

How are you going to explore relaxation, sleep, healthy eating, home comforts and self-care?

How will you begin to raise self-esteem with affirmation and acknowledgement of achievements, looking at constant change and progress?

WORKSHEET

Self-Appraisal

What are your main qualities as a person?

What are your strengths?

What do you believe you are good at?

What are you confident in?

What are the things you like about yourself?

Mapping out your own vicious cycles of low self-esteem

What is keeping your low self-esteem going?

There is always a trigger to keeping low self-esteem going, so it is important to find your trigger/s and challenge/change them to help break these patterns of behaviour.

Example:

Trigger – Interview having high expectations of self to get this job you want.

Negative predictions – There are a lot of people going for the job. I am not good enough or qualified enough.

Unhelpful behaviour – Putting pressure on oneself, not getting enough sleep the night before, feeling that you must work harder/try harder.

Self-critical thoughts – Why am I bothering to try so hard when I am not going to get the job anyway? It is a waste of my time.

Consequences on feelings – Anxiety – headache, sweating, upset tummy. Depression – feeling hopeless, low, avoiding people, doing nothing.

WORKSHEET

What are your triggers?

What are your negative predictions?

What are your unhelpful behaviours?

What are your self-critical thoughts?

What are the consequences for your feelings?

Getting SMART/ A plan of action

When devising an action plan, it is important to ensure that what you plan to do will get you where you want to go. If your plan is too ambitious, you may not be able to put it into practice successfully, and this is likely to discourage and demoralise you. If your plan is vague, you may find that after a week or month or two you may forget the initial idea of what you are supposed to be doing.

If your plan is too limited, you may feel as if you are not making any real progress towards becoming the person you want to be. So, whichever stage you are at – first or second or final draft – ensure your action plan meets the SMART criteria:

S – is simple and specific enough

M – is measurable

A – is agreed

R – is it realistic?

T – is it timescale reasonable?

Time to reflect on your learning and set your own personal goals:

Example: I want to learn to play an instrument

S – Start thinking about the instrument that you would like to play, cost, time, etc.

M – Take time to measure the goal and reflect on progress.

A – Ask is this achievable, or do I need to take stock each month?

R – Can I realistically achieve this goal? How am I doing?

T – Do I need to move the timescale to ensure I reach my goal?

Problem solving/Goal setting

Successful goal setting

Goal setting is much respected, and often poorly practised. As a source of self-esteem based on performance, it is immensely powerful. It maximises the chances of behavioural success and provides an excellent mechanism for recognising success through feedback. Many of the problems that arise with goal setting, however, derive from several sources that it is important to address in advance.

The most common are:
- Poor choice of goals (particularly unrealistic goals)
- Underestimation of timescale and obstacles to achieve goals
- Poor perseverance/practice with goal setting and fear of failure

1 Goal choice: estimation of goals can be difficult for the practised, let alone unpractised, goal setter. The importance of setting achievable goals is the key to success. Visualisation, descriptive or art techniques may be useful in enabling you to achieve the result.
2 Underestimation of timescale and obstacles, goal completion can often take longer than we think and longer than we would want. Encouraging realistic timescales and giving leeway to potential obstacles in advance to decide whether, when and how they are to be tackled, plus the necessary resources, is especially important.
3 Poor perseverance and practice; all long journeys, especially those involving obstacles, involve development of strategies that maximise our chances of persevering. The most common involve addressing potential obstacles as indicated above, taking frequent breaks, recognising the downsides of giving up, reflecting on how far we have travelled, reflecting on the next stage of the journey, its obstacles and how to tackle them. Enjoying the scenery at certain stop-off points, giving ourselves treats and energy boosters at times of low morale.

The more a person practises goal setting, the easier the perseverance becomes. Equally, to see failure at an early stage is to normalise it, see it as a crucial element of success, and to emphasise that failure is a statement of attempt, while those who never try at all are the only people who fail.

Start an exercise in setting goals while also recognising the need to incorporate achievable goals.

Plan of Action
How did your low self-esteem develop?

What kept it going?

What are your key unhelpful thoughts and beliefs?

What positive alternatives do you have for them?

How can you build on what you have learnt?

What might lead to a setback for you?

If you do have a setback, what will you do about it?

MY POSITIVE STATEMENT TO MYSELF IS:

Planning the future

Putting your learning into practice:

How you treat yourself impacts on how the world perceives you and how you develop relationships.

When having the tools to develop your self-esteem and practising your knowledge, you can then move forward to lead a healthier, happier life.

The above takes regular practice and, like most human beings, you will sometimes revert to what is most common. However, in time, with practice, you will make the changes you want to make and continue to develop more positive relationships.

Everything in life starts and ends with you. If you allow people to treat you in a manner that is not respectful or kind, they will continue to do this as they will feel this is what you expect. Your body language may also tell a person how you feel about yourself.

Having better self-awareness and being kind to self, you may be surprised how quickly your experiences in life change. People will begin to treat you differently; they will appreciate you more as well as be kinder to you.

Understanding that being assertive is not anger and being kind is not a weakness. This will allow you to communicate your feelings better, and people will respond to you in a more authentic manner.

The more authentic we are, the more we allow others to be.

Valuing yourself also allows you to value others. Quietening our critical voice allows us to see others as they truly are as well as allowing ourselves to be who we are.

JUST WHEN THE CATERPILLAR THOUGHT THEIR WORLD WAS OVER, THEY BECAME A BUTTERFLY.

Chapter Twelve

REBECCA'S JOURNEY

(Rebecca–female, late teens)

Rebecca came to counselling due to concerns from her family and partner about her eating. She had not been diagnosed with an eating disorder but during the pandemic she found herself becoming quite obsessive about her weight and the food she put into her body. She was restricting food and had the belief that she was fat. Rebecca informed me that her mother had struggled with an eating disorder – bulimia – most of her life and that her father presented with obsessive behaviours and rituals. She was an only child, had a good relationship with both parents and was in a relationship with a partner who was both supportive and kind.

Rebecca presented as extremely low weight and often wore clothes that were a lot larger than her body. We initially explored her eating patterns, the beginning of her eating issues and what had triggered this. Rebecca shared her experiences growing up in a house with a mother with an eating disorder and the need to count calories. She also identified an anxiety/fear of what would happen if she ate normally. Rebecca wanted to explore her value of worth, her reasons for what she regarded as self-harm and her learnt experiences. She is an intelligent young woman who had a sense of herself as well as the unhelpful behaviours she engaged in.

We initially explored what triggered her restriction of food, her internal dialogue, her rituals, behaviours and view of self. Rebecca stated she was ready to explore all aspects and areas of her behaviour; however, there were times when she appeared to feel quite challenged by my encouragement and for me to know what her routine was. Once trust had been built within the relationship, everything changed.

As I worked with Rebecca, she identified a lack of value and talked through her negative thoughts about herself as well as the impact this had on her behaviour. Rebecca was able to identify labels and messages from her past that had recently returned during the pandemic, and which had impacted on her self-image.

When Rebecca began to do the work on raising her value of self, implementing steps and practising challenging her thoughts, change occurred. She soon began to realise that she had choices/options and began to really appreciate the people around her who gave her support; friends, partner, family, etc. She became more honest to herself about what she had been doing with food, why and how she felt.

Rebecca revealed feelings of anxiety, often questioning herself and comparing self to others. Picking holes in who she was and how she looked. Rebecca had a good understanding of her learning from her mother regarding food and counting calories, but once she realised she could do things differently and that it did not have to be the same, she started the process of changing.

We began by exploring her relationship with food, her understanding of why she did the things she did, what changes she wanted to make, her support network and how she could utilise others as a support. Rebecca worked through various worksheets to build her self-awareness and as tools for change. She began to build her self-worth, practise affirmations, implement new routines, buy new clothes, wear more fitted clothes, increase her appetite for food and enjoy the food she ate.

In short, she began to like who she was as a person and how she looked. She began to wear clothes that were more colourful and fitted, more revealing, showing more confidence in herself and how she looked. She began to receive praise from people around her who noticed the changes. She questioned and challenged her negative thoughts and began to implement new ones. She worked hard both inside and outside the therapy room as she appeared determined to make the changes she wanted to make.

When working with Rebecca, one of the things I noticed from the beginning was her motivation to change, but somehow through her thinking or comparing herself to others, she had become caught in a net of confusion and questioning. Once she realised that she could just be herself and start accepting this, she continued to make positive changes. I saw the confident woman underneath the anxious self-critical person that initially came to see me, which is who she is today. Not only confident and self-assured but with self-worth and value.

Experience as written by Rebecca

During lockdown, I felt extremely out of control, so I decided to start going for runs but then started to lose weight and feel so proud of myself. But then because I was not eating enough, I could not run anymore because I did not have any energy. So instead of running, I then restricted my intake of food more throughout lockdown to carry on losing weight and still get that feeling of worth. Then when coming to university, I had no parents to sneak food around or pretend that I was eating to, so the restriction got worse and worse.

This was until my boyfriend and my flatmate started to notice me progressively eating less and getting smaller and decided to speak to me about it. I just cried because I did not really know how to say that I needed help. I started with counselling through university, but it was not much help; they did not have anyone that could specifically help me with my eating. After going to the doctor's and getting results back that I did not expect and that scared me and my friends and family, I decided I really wanted to get better for me. I started by making a meal plan for the week, just increasing slightly, and I remember feeling petrified at the amount. But now I look back and I am so proud of how far I have come. Susan has really helped me lessen my anxiety around food by helping me pinpoint any triggers around. Then finding out that when I am stressed, it is my intake that takes the hit to compensate for wanting to be in control.

Susan has helped me to see that I am a young lady that really does deserve to be happy and eat without guilt, and even though there are always going to be some down days, I am immensely proud of how far I have come and can now tackle these down days better. I remember looking in the mirror during lockdown and in my first year at university and hating what I looked like all the time, constantly weighing myself and feeling guilty if the number did not go down. But with Susan's help, I do not hate what I see in the mirror anymore. Even after putting on weight since, I feel more confident in my body than before, and I can look in the mirror and say that I love my body for everything it does for me, and I should love it. There are days when I do not feel this confidence and want to hide my body, but I try my best to not let it affect me or what I wear. Susan has helped me realise that there is more to life than constantly trying to shrink myself.

Chapter Thirteen

NINA'S JOURNEY
(Nina–female, mid-teens)

When asked if I would like to write about myself in this book, I responded with laughter. This was because, when considering, I found myself confronted with the thought that my story is not good enough to be in a book. This reflects the whole concept of what we are talking about - self-esteem, and so my answer was clear. I think the journey of loving yourself is lifelong, but the process allows you to utterly understand yourself and how you want to live your life.

Growing up, we are told of the commodities that make us valuable: intelligence, beauty, talent. We are told that the value lies within ourselves; we are not told of the tools that feed validation. Validation is a key word in this. It is what many of us determine our self-worth from as we live in a society where we feel we are only as good as what people see us to be. I speak of this subject as if I am at a good place with myself, which I must confirm is not true. I am only at the start of my journey, which starts with understanding and embracing. This may seem painful and unnecessary if there is no quick fix, but there can be no healing without understanding. This started when I began therapy with Susan. At first, it just seemed like a time each week when I could express what I thought without feeling judged or receiving horrified looks. However, these absolute truths in my mind, embedded in my addiction, began to unfold within therapy, and I was able to start acknowledging the reality behind them. This enabled me to separate my true self of love, kindness and creativity from 'the gremlin' (as Susan calls it) of suffering, hatred and abuse that exists within us as humans.

Self-esteem I believe to be the foundation that determines how we live our lives. For many of us, the foundation is weak and rotting into the soil. However, this is not visible from the house in which we live above. Our enjoyment of life is dependent on how we value ourselves; it dictates the nature of our thoughts, actions, habits and relationships. In society, the relationship that we have with ourselves is very much subconscious and

often not embodied as we run round in circles causing harm to ourselves
without understanding why. For me, this was in an eating disorder. When
active in my illness, I had no concept of my self-esteem or how it was
affecting me. It is something so deep within us, which makes it often
inaccessible. I could not explain to anyone why I would do such a thing
to myself. At the time, there was no explanation; there did not need to be.
It felt right; it felt it had purpose and validated something deep within me
– what I now know to be my flagging self-esteem. Causing such pain to
myself felt addictive and fulfilling to the point where I had no concept of
the real world. I had destroyed the relationship with my family and home;
I had been taken out of school and hobbies and could not walk out of the
house as it was too strenuous. Thinking about this now, I can see
objectively what a terrible existence that was, but when deeply immersed
in these cycles, there is not much that can steer you out. The pain only
fuelled my behaviour because that is all I was after at the end of the day.
Like most, my eating disorder stemmed in the form of body image.
Through the entire course of it, I hated my body and so I was doing
something about it. However, these thoughts circling of ugly, fat, repulsive,
disgusting when I look in the mirror, I see them embedded in my low self-
worth and my body is just the projection of them. I used present tense
there as my body is still something I feel uncomfortable with and generates
many negative thoughts about myself, but the difference is that I am now
in the process of healing that relationship, not fuelling the fire. In doing
this, I find it helpful to remove the entire concept of society and other
people when looking at my body and instead spend time thinking about
how incredible it is and what it does for us as humans. It is a completely
incomprehensible system that acts as our home and vessel to experience
the world. From this perspective, the size and shape of the body becomes
insignificant, and it becomes something to cherish and love, not to hurt.
We tend to view our body and mind as separate, our mind telling us that
we hate our body but, in fact, they are one. Our body is us, not a separate
entity that can be isolated and abused. When this happens, we are hurting
ourselves, not 'our body'. This is where the misconception of eating
disorders being purely based on body image arises, because, in fact, our
actions of abuse are in fight against our entire being.

Learning to love oneself and feel comfortable in our own skin does not
come with a list of set- out instructions and a rule book. When I first

started recovery (reluctantly), I did not think it would ever be possible to get to where I am now. The thought of it terrified me and I honestly believed my life would be a short futile existence, and because I could not love myself, that thought did not seem particularly distressing. My experience was exasperated by the UK treatment system for eating disorders, which I found worsened my state of despair. Some people find them helpful, depending on who you work with personally within the institution. For me, I found the time extremely damaging as I felt treated punitively, as if what I was doing was merely a choice, and I was a terrible person for choosing to hurt those around me. I experienced their techniques as threatening; slowly, one by one removing the sources of enjoyment in my life in the hope of propelling me to eat. I can confirm this did not work. Not once was I asked about why I felt the need to hurt myself; not once was I given the love that I so desperately needed. The experience only degraded my self-esteem further by enforcing the ideas that I was foolish, selfish and to blame for the chaos that surrounded me. At this point, I became suicidal, which I must mention my treatment team were aware of but did not acknowledge or address. My parents could see that the treatment was only worsening my state and decided to take a risk and manage it within the family, under the condition that if I was to get worse, we would have to return to treatment. This is where I can now realise how crucial the treatment service provided to me was in my recovery. The experience of being under their control was and still is so traumatic that it functioned as a motivating force as I was so desperate to never return. So, in this sense, it is useful due to how horrific it is. However, I really hope that the treatment system is revolutionised so that people suffering with eating disorders can and will be treated with love, care and compassion at a time when they are struggling to find that within themselves.

Working alliance

When I first started working with Nina, she presented as bubbly, bright and outgoing, although she had a history of anorexia. She had a good awareness of her feelings and appeared quite well practised at masking her feelings. This was indicative of someone who had been hurt so badly that they no longer knew who to trust. We started to build our relationship slowly, getting to know each other, laughing, building a space of comfort/safety without pressure, with acceptance, respect, value of the person and their process.

We worked creatively, exploring her knowledge of herself, wants, needs and abilities. As an artist, Nina was able to visualise her experience as well as give colour and pictures to allow me to see what she wanted to say in her own way as well as begin to understand her processes. Nina is an intelligent, aware young person, who has a sensitivity to the world around her which allows her to have compassion as well as empathy for her fellow humans. She is incredibly talented, which can come with additional pressures and impact on her experiences as well as her view of the world. Working with her has allowed me to work visually, creatively, mindfully and flexibly but most of all ensure she is seen and heard fully at all times. Nina's experiences of treatment for her anorexia appeared to have left her scarred, scared and traumatised, as well as leading to a mistrust of any kind of therapy. I feel that she did incredibly well throughout the entire process of our work, taking into consideration her past experiences. She also gave herself space and time in allowing our relationship to develop. I valued our relationship and time working together. I found her to be incredibly strong, brave, intuitive, talented and kind.

Chapter Fourteen

ANXIETY AND LOW SELF-ESTEEM (ADDITIONAL MINDFULNESS)

I have brought anxiety, low self-esteem and mindfulness together in this chapter as a way of making sense of the actions and what you can do. Firstly, recognising the correlation between anxiety and low self-esteem then looking at the action of using mindfulness to reduce the anxiety and therefore decrease negative self-talk in the hope of increasing self-esteem.

The correlation between anxiety and low self-esteem is the perpetuation of negative thoughts/behaviours leading to increased anxiety and often depression.

If our internal dialogue is consistently negative, then it makes sense that it will then affect how we feel, which subsequently increases a low self-image and therefore low self-esteem.

People with low self-esteem often have a problematic past, and anxiety is the brain's attempt to do something about the negative repetitive thought process.

Anxiety is a mental and physical reaction to perceived threats. In small doses, it can be helpful as it protects us from harm/danger and focuses our attention; however, too frequently, it can be debilitating.

Cognitive distortions are irrational thoughts influencing our emotions and behaviours. In the extreme, they can be harmful.

Overthinking things

Rumination is:

- Dwelling on difficulties and things that distress us
- Repeatedly thinking about events of the past
- Becoming preoccupied with something and not being able to get it out of your mind
- A learnt strategy for trying to deal with our problems

The problems with rumination are:

- Unhelpful rumination tends to focus on causes and consequences instead of solution

- Tends to focus on what has gone wrong, leading to negative thinking
- When used excessively can lead to depression
- Overdone, it can lead to inactivity and avoidance of problem solving

Rumination is natural as thinking about problems can be helpful in reaching a solution. Most people ruminate for a limited time when problem solving, although, if excessive, rumination can become problematic.

Anxiety can lead to the following:
Look at the list below and see if you can identify with any of them. Then complete the questions on the next sheet by explaining why and how you do these.

Magnification – Exaggerating or minimising the importance of events
Catastrophising – Seeing only the worst possible outcomes
Magical thinking – The belief that acts will influence unrelated situations
Personalisation – The belief that one is responsible for events outside of their control
Jumping to conclusions – Interpreting the meaning of a situation with no or little evidence
Mind reading – Interpreting the thoughts and beliefs of others without evidence
Fortune telling – The belief that a situation will turn out badly with no evidence
Should statements – The belief that things should be a certain way
All or nothing – Thinking in absolutes. Always, never or every.

WORKSHEET

Do you magnify situations and events? If so, how?

Do you catastrophise? When and how?

Are you a magical thinker? In what way?

Do you make situations and events about you?

Taking on the responsibility?

Why do you think you do this?

Are you someone that jumps to conclusions? Is this useful for you?

Do you think you can mind read what others are thinking? In what situations?

Are you someone that feels that you can fortune tell? When and why?

Do you think that things should be a certain way? Why?

WORKSHEET

Anxiety, as we know, can be debilitating. If struggling with anxiety, it is a good idea to explore why this is happening, what your triggers are and how you can help reduce the anxiety.

Can you think of three things that might trigger your anxiety?

What are your physical symptoms when anxious?

Can you identify three thoughts when anxious?

How do you cope when anxious?

What are the things that you do?

Breathing, Mindfullness and Self-Esteem

We know through research today that addictive patterns such as overeating or smoking reduce with mindfulness, and the quality of a person's connections improve. People's brain patterns can change when they learn mindfulness. Certain schools of thought believe that after only eight weeks of actively doing a mindfulness course, people display a shift in activity from the right to the left prefrontal cortex, correlating with less anxiety and depression. Changes in the brain occur, including thickening in regions of the brain associated with memory, emotion regulation, self-awareness and perspective-taking.

Mindfulness breathing covers four foundations, beginning with attention to breathing, watching, feeling the breath and how it anchors the mind, giving the mind something to stay with and return to.

Before I commenced my training in mindfulness, the first book I read was Ed Halliwell's Into the Heart of Mindfulness, a man's journey of depression and anxiety and how mindfulness helped him make positive changes in his life. I had already had experience of meditation, but this was not always consistent or structured. Through this book, I began to notice the breath, practise and pay attention. It was through his encouragement I noticed how often I paid attention to where the mind tended to go, patterns of being lost in thought, emotions and sensations. By training the mind to return repeatedly to the present, to anchor the breath in the body, I gradually enabled stability to develop.

Anxiety and the impact of meditation – just taking small steps by building up meditation times from seconds to minutes rather than starting at five to ten minutes can help, without leaving you feeling overwhelmed. When working with clients, I usually start with a few seconds of mindfulness and build from there, especially with those who are particularly anxious.

You can start your journey into mindfulness by either mindful drinking or mindful eating. Mindful tea-drinking can start as a challenge to drink one cup a day, paying attention to all the sensations of taste, touch and smell, and returning to these whenever you notice your mind descend into tangles of thought. I have encouraged people to use this technique, and it has been extremely helpful as a starting point of meditation. All below can also be achieved when eating food, taking the time to notice the sight, smell, touch, taste, etc.

The practice of mindful tea-drinking:
- Paying attention
- Noticing the feeling!
- Pouring the tea
- Lifting the tea bag
- Adding the milk/sugar
- Noticing the temperature!
- The taste
- The swallowing
- The movement of the tea in the body
- The thoughts that try to stop this process
- Your eyes and your surroundings
- Returned attention to the cup

Mindfulness works by focusing our attention on the present moment; it counteracts rumination and worrying. Worrying about the future. What is happening next, what the day might bring, external things like bills to pay, etc., and ruminating about the past. I wish this did not happen, why did I do that? etc. Of course, it is important to learn from our past and make plans; however, when we spend too much time outside of the present moment, we can get depressed and anxious. Mindfulness can be a valuable tool for helping us to focus better on the present moment.

Research has shown that mindfulness helps us reduce anxiety and depression. Mindfulness teaches us how to respond to stress with awareness of what is happening in the present moment, rather than simply acting instinctively, unaware of what emotions or motives may be driving that decision. By teaching awareness for one's physical and mental state in the moment, mindfulness allows for more adaptive reactions to tricky situations.

Mindfulness works in several ways. It encourages us to be open and accept our emotions. As a result, we are better able to identify, experience and process them. Mindfulness also encourages us to see things from different perspectives. For example, if your spouse/partner/friend snaps at you, you might blame yourself and worry that you have done something to upset them. If you can distance yourself from your immediate response of feeling hurt, you might remember that they mentioned having had a difficult day, and they snapped at you because they are tired or stressed and/or feeling unhappy.

The practice of mindfulness has been known to benefit the following areas:

- **Body awareness:** Body awareness is the ability to notice subtle sensations in the body and self-report findings that mindfulness leads to greater perceptions of body awareness. Being aware of your internal emotional state is necessary for the ability to better regulate those emotions.
- **Focused attention:** Mindfulness practice improves one's ability to focus attention. Neuroimaging studies have shown that mindfulness increases activation in the anterior cingulate cortex, a brain area that is involved in executive function and attention. Through better control of attention, it can be easier to focus on a present task rather than be distracted by worry.
- **Self-perception:** Mindfulness also changes one's perspective of oneself. Buddhist psychology teaches that the self is not permanent and static but a combination of ongoing mental events. Two months of mindfulness meditation practices has been known to increase self-esteem and self-acceptance.
- **Physical health:** Mindfulness meditation has also been known to produce other health benefits, such as reduced blood pressure and cortisol levels (stress hormone).

Mindfulness practice

There is no big secret behind mindfulness practices. Any activity can become mindful by focusing on the experience of the present moment. For example, you can either mindlessly walk along a path or take a little bit of time and practise mindful walking by looking around and noticing things; the different trees, flowers, people, mindfully taking your environment in. Not surprisingly, it is much more enjoyable and satisfying when you take time to appreciate your surroundings than when you walk mindlessly. Interestingly, you will also notice that you will enjoy the walks more when walking mindfully.

There are many practices that include mindfulness trainings, such as tai chi, yoga and zen. There are many styles for each of these activities, so it is worthwhile experimenting with different practices until you find one that suits you. As you become more mindful, you will also notice that you will become more centred, happier and less depressed, and this in turn has a direct positive effect on your anxiety.

How to be mindful right now

Focus on your breath for a few minutes. Feel your chest rise and fall; notice the sensation of the breath as it enters and exits your nose. When your mind wanders, simply return your attention to the breath. Focus on the present moment: the here and now. Notice this very moment; it feels good to be alive, right now.

If you do not immediately feel a complete release of anxiety, remember most of the benefits of mindfulness require consistent practice. While some changes bolster against anxiety even after one single yoga class, most benefits require several weeks, months and even years to create a noticeable change. And, like any skill, you will need to continue to practise mindfulness after you start, to maintain the improvements.

Making mindfulness part of your life will only bring improvements and reduce stress. Like anything, the challenge is to practise and implement it into your life. In the past couple of years, I began training in mindfulness firstly as a participant, and then as a teacher I can feel the benefits even more. I have had good self-awareness for many years with my training as a counsellor, but mindfulness has brought another perspective in really tuning in to how I am feeling in the moment and really being present in that moment, which is truly magical. It feels like time is slowing down and my life has become longer as I have more time to do all the things I love as well as work, which is amazing.

The Practice of the Body Scan

The body scan is a foundational practice of mindfulness courses. This can be practised lying down. The prime intention of this is to incline the mind into a sensory experience to become aware of how it is to 'be a body'.

Lying down, preferably on a firm surface – using a mat or blanket. It is a time for you to let go of time into a stillness, to feel yourself held by the earth. Feeling the sensations of the body, 'how does it feel lying there right now?'

Bringing your attention to the inhalation and exhalation of your breath. Imagine dropping an anchor into the breath, your attention placed gently on to the rhythm of the breath, riding the waves that ebb and flow within you. Initially concentrating only on the breath flowing in and out of the body.

Starting from the bottom of the body, noticing the sensations in your left toes, moving the mind's eye down into the part of the body, noticing the sensations. There is no need to do anything but observe the sensations in the body. Being aware of any changes in sensations and any tendencies to try to hold on to them or push them away.

You can also synchronise what you are sensing with the rhythm of your breath by breathing into the left toe on each in-breath and breathing out from the toe on each out-breath. You may notice thoughts and reactions arising as you practise. This is not a problem, and there is no need to try to alter or get rid of them. At the same time, as you are practising paying attention to the body sensations, allow yourself to let go of following these thoughts and reactions. When you notice your attention has wandered into thought, or is following an impulse, or has drifted to a different part of the body, you might acknowledge that this wandering has occurred, then gently return your attention back to your toes.

Open your awareness now to the top of the left foot, resting with the sensations in this region for a while. Now offer a friendly presence to the bottom of the foot, and to the heel; gradually work your way up through the leg, ankle, lower leg, knee, and so on. Giving attention over to the sensations that arise in these regions.

Gently and carefully work your attention to your whole body in this way: hips, pelvic region, back, shoulders, each arm and hand, belly, chest, neck and head. Gently acknowledge the mind wandering and notice it. Let this be an opportunity to practise kindness, patience and conscious choice, as you bring the attention back to the sensations in the region of the body you are working with.

When you have scanned the entire body, let your attention open out to notice all the body's sensations and let them feel held in kindly awareness.

WORKSHEET

How can you begin to bring mindfulness into your life?

What action would you need to take for the above to happen?

What are your blocks for bringing mindfulness meditations into your life?

What are your concerns, if any?

How will you begin?

What next ...?

I initially started meditating in the early 1990s; however, I found long meditations did not work for me, and sitting in silence was a trigger to encourage my fast thought process. It took me years and many attempts to finally find guided meditations that started with short focus, then moving on to guided meditations that I built up slowly over time. I found it challenging to just sit with myself and be quiet as I was an anxious person back then, often living in the future, not in the present. My mind was often ahead of me, always thinking about what next and how I get there. When working with people who have anxiety and who have never meditated, I tend to start very slowly, concentrating on the breath, encouraging them to get a sense of how they may feel. I meditate daily as part of my regular routine and often implement an extra short meditation during my working day just to check in with myself and notice how I am in the present. I also do a mindful walk every day, allowing myself to live in the now, noticing things around me; sounds, smells, visualisation. This anchors me as well as allowing me to be and live in the present.

My experience of meditation and now using mindfulness has helped me live in a more relaxed way, less worry or stress more present in that moment of that day. I have become more aware of my life, how I live it, more honest about my wants/needs. I can put myself first in what I want, not in a selfish way, but putting me first, doing my meditation in the morning, having breakfast, exercising or going for a walk allows me to be able to focus on the work with others in their time and allows me to have the space, time and energy for them. I do not get resentful about meeting the needs of others or working hard for the people I support. I have the time and the energy for each person and can be creative with the work we do together. Meditation and mindfulness have allowed me to create a space totally for me, giving me a better awareness of myself, the world and others, as well as being able to share those experiences with others.

Meditation and mindfulness have now become a way of life for me, learning something new each day about myself, my body, my relationships, my time and work. Having a structure in my day whereby mindfulness is part of that structure, giving me a different, more real, sense of self. I was once a highly anxious person, always putting pressure on myself to be perfect! Very driven and fast. I did not sleep through the night until I was forty years old as my mind was so overactive all the time and alert, due to past trauma. I used to live in the future, never in the present, not appreciating life in the now! I was too busy doing to see what was going on in the present and had no real sense of how I was feeling. Mindfulness has completely changed how I live in my life today, and with lifelong practice it will continue to do so, and my hope is that it will support others too.

Chapter Fifteen

CHLOE'S JOURNEY
(Chloe–female, eighteen years)

Client late teens, just completing her A levels and exploring university options. Chloe is a highly intelligent young lady with a good understanding of human psychology. She has compassion as well as empathy for others and a mindful approach to the sensitivity of others; however, this did not initially relate to herself.

Chloe came to see me at the end of the pandemic due to the impact of the pandemic on her self-esteem as well as having noticed levels of anxiety that had also impacted on her relationships within school. Chloe asked for support in understanding her feelings and wanted to explore what she could do to support change. She stated that she was finding it hard to assert herself in relation to others, who were sometimes undermining her abilities and qualities as a human being. She struggled with her relationships and finding her voice among certain peers. When exploring a pattern, the client became aware that what she was experiencing was similar to an early experience that had continued in her present life. Her initial experience was with extended family members who often talked over her and used their loudness as a way of gaining control of situations, as well as the possible use of intimidating behaviour.

We worked together, providing a place of safety and trust as well as equality as human beings. She gradually built a relationship with me whereby she began to transform both physically and emotionally, finding her voice in a more confident way, recognising changes as time went on. We worked together on building confidence, exploring how to value oneself as well as how to have a voice without needing to be loud. She was able to practise within the sessions what she wanted to say to others, as well as experience how she wanted to have value, particularly from her peers, and within a matter of a few months the client's relationships, particularly within her school, began to change. She acknowledged that by making changes within herself, people responded to her differently. She noticed that as she changed certain behaviours, as well as her body language, the other girls within her group stopped making negative comments towards her and the teasing initially reduced, eventually stopping.

Chloe realised that through her experiences with her extended family and not allowing herself space to have a voice, she continued to create this pattern within other relationships, which left her feeling worthless and of little value. Once she had recognised the patterns that she repeated and began to respond differently, her self-esteem and confidence began to grow and she continued to practise assertion. Using the tools and strategies that worked for her enabled change to occur, as well as practising these new ways of being; the client began to recognise and value her worth. Chloe is continuing to practise her newfound worth until these changes become her new way of being.

Working alliance

Like many clients, Chloe was a joy to work with as she had a good understanding of herself and a good awareness of the impact of her low self-esteem on her life. Her motivation to want to change and be more assertive in particular encouraged my support. She is an intelligent, thoughtful young woman who often put others' feelings before herself, leaving her without the energy or time to take care of her own needs. She had a sense of humour and a gentle character which left her feeling unheard and disrespected at times, especially from some members of her group of friends. Each week, she would want to explore and address her experiences, practising the changes she wanted to make and feeding back how people responded to these changes. It could often be a challenge for her in particular to receive acknowledgement from family; however, some of her close friends were able to acknowledge and praise her for the changes she had made. Being of a similar culture, we were able to use humour within the therapeutic relationship, meeting each other through our culture but also acknowledging the negatives about the use of humour at times. I found her to be engaging, motivated, someone who was keen to learn and open to new ways of being. I enjoyed our time together as well as being able to see her needs/wants, but without making them obvious, so she had to work them out for herself. Watching, giving space to grow and making the changes at her pace, in her time and how she wanted was not only to be a part of but was also a pride for me to see her growth. Chloe went from being intimidated by other females who were both disrespectful and unkind to asserting her needs, informing those people of her choice not to continue a friendship and heading off to another city for university.

Chapter Sixteen

FORGIVENESS, GRATITUDE AND THE IMPACT ON SELF-ESTEEM

Research has shown that those who practise self-forgiveness have better mental health and wellbeing, more positive relationships, higher productivity, success, focus and concentration. Learning to self-forgive takes practice and allows the person to have a more open, happy, relaxed life.

A person with high self-esteem appears to forgive more easily, whereas a person with low self-esteem seems to blame. Forgiveness comes in many forms and stages – remorse, responsibility, compassion and motivation. There is always a learning within these processes, and when one is open to learn about themselves and others through forgiveness, the healing can take place.

Forgiveness for me is about letting go of all the hurts, allowing self to be free, and not holding on to toxic resentments which would cause harm to the mind and body.

I used to call it collecting straws whereby I was holding or harbouring thoughts, feelings and anger towards others due to them either not meeting my needs/expectations or by an event/situation from the past that caused me to feel hurt.

When we are unforgiving, we can appear or present as victims of other people's unacceptable behaviour. The victim mentality can grow over time, building a list in a person's mind, increasing resentment and anger inside themselves. Forgiveness releases these negative feelings, demonstrating growth and maturity, freeing us from the vicious cycles we create for ourselves. I am not saying it is easy to forgive, especially if other people's behaviour/actions have had a detrimental impact on your life; nonetheless, there are times when it is important to think about the bigger picture as our actions and words impact on our lives/wellbeing.

Our experiences do not define us as we all make mistakes (being human), so hanging on to the past does absolutely no good for anyone. I believe forgiveness can truly set us free, to make peace with our past and create a better future for ourselves.

I believe that holding on to the past and harbouring ill feelings can only keep us stuck, creates bitterness and can make us sick. It is easy to say but with practice and support it is important to let go of past negative experiences and free yourself from the pain of holding on to it. There is nothing to gain from holding on to old feelings. This will only keep the person in the victim role whereby the view of the world then becomes distorted, seeing others as persecutors whereby you then may look for people to rescue you or protect you as you feel unable to do this for yourself. When using the term victim, I do not mean this in a negative way as we learn the role as a defensive mechanism and way to survive situations. I remained in that role for a long time as it was what I knew and how I learnt to survive certain situations.

When I look back on my experiences of being a victim for many years but not realising it, I blamed others for the way I was, how I behaved and what I thought about myself. Once I learnt that letting go of resentment could free me and enable me to be whatever, however, I wanted/wished to be, I began the process of letting go. I would make myself a list of all the people who I felt had caused me harm, had a negative effect on my life or had not been kind to me and gradually worked through, forgiving them.

I then worked through that list of forgiveness by looking at their lives, those that I knew of, and seeing how patterns repeated themselves; my parents, ex-partners, family members, friends, etc. I did not give reasons for their behaviours, but I made sense of it, putting the responsibility where it should be but no longer harbouring ill feelings so that I could free myself.

Forgiveness of all took several years as I had an extensive list to get through. Although most were easy, the one that took the longest was an ex-partner who was incredibly abusive. I cannot quite explain it, but he felt caught in my body, and I struggled to let him go. I explored why he was stuck there and how toxic it was for me to still carry these feelings. I initially worked through the anger and how destructive I was being towards myself, causing harm, repeating the abuse, then finally, one day, I let him go. Phew! There was a massive relief, a freedom that I cannot begin to explain. He had not been in my thoughts for years until I started authoring this book, but now when I think of him or that time, I feel calm as I have been able to make sense of his behaviour, knowing his past and family dynamics. I have also forgiven him fully and found a place for compassion/empathy for both him and my younger self during that time.

By harbouring or holding on to old resentments and anger towards others, we can imprison ourselves, causing ourselves harm, while the people/person is getting on with their own lives and may be causing harm to someone else. It does not resolve the situation, nor does it relieve us from past hurts but may get stuck inside us, creating all number of harms and ailments. Releasing the people/person who may have contributed to you feeling harmed is allowing yourself freedom of choice. Forgiving others for causing you harm takes time and can be more challenging; however, if you are able to do this then healing has begun.

I believe everyone has a reason for their behaviours, and I try to find compassion for all those people. I know some have had difficult childhoods and may have experienced abuse of some kind, therefore not having experience of care or affirmation, even feeling love in their lives will have had an impact on how they behave towards others.

We all need the space to feel loved, cared for, nurtured, affirmed; otherwise, it can impact on our relationships and how we relate to one another. I feel strongly about this and would encourage anyone who has had difficult dynamics or lack of love in their family to work through this in therapy to then be able to have a dissimilar experience; otherwise, we just keep repeating patterns of our parents or caregivers, and nothing changes. First, it is important to become aware of our behaviour and the impact on others, be willing to make changes, then seek help to change. I am not saying this is an easy journey, but we are all worth it and deserve a chance to have a better life.

I believe that had I not forgiven or thought about those people who I believed caused me harm then I would be carrying them with me today. Carrying the anger, fear, resentment, hurt, which in turn would no doubt impact on my relationships with new people in my life and continue to do so.

Forgiveness of self – this can be even more challenging than forgiving others. Interesting statement but true. I remember how I blamed myself for many things I had not done, said, achieved, for how others had treated me and how I treated myself.

Forgiveness of self

It was interesting for me to explore this one as this was the hardest of them all. It took time, patience and love over a period of years to forgive my younger self for putting me in dangerous situations, my experience of sexual assaults, my drinking as a younger person and the mistakes I made within relationships. I know of course now that it was all a part of my learning and experiences that led to these things happening. If I did not have such low self-worth, I would have felt I had a voice and would not have tried to fit in so hard or have found myself in situations that I could not get out of through fear or helplessness. As a child, I was neither protected from abuse nor experienced feelings of safety. As a teen, I could not rely on others to keep me safe, so I was sexually assaulted and left with the shame as well as blame within myself. As an adult, I continued to either accept abusive behaviour or found myself in vulnerable situations to be abused, although I was aware of repetitive patterns, why things happened the way that they did and the reasons behind my behaviour. I still needed to find a way to change. I do not blame myself or anyone else for what happened, but I have made sense of the situations and events along the way. I wish none of the situations had happened and feel sad when I think about my younger self and those challenges, but I no longer hold any anger, resentment or hatred towards me or anyone else. There are reasons for everything, and I fully understand them today and have found forgiveness for all.

I was born at a time when abuse did not appear to be recognised as it is today. Children were not protected, and women were sexualised and repeatedly abused by men (#MeToo).

Whenever my thoughts connect with the past, especially when authoring this book in particular as it has brought me back to memories that were painful, I reassure myself that none of it was my fault and comfort that part of me by regulation and reassurance. I also feel that without some of those experiences, I would not be the woman I am today, so I have learnt a lot and experienced a lot for a reason, which in turn helps others survive and heal from their wounds.

I know today, and have done for some time, that I am a woman who is a survivor. I am strong, hopeful, optimistic and resourceful.

When exploring all of the above and how a lack of forgiveness impacts on one's self esteem, you may see that it just keeps us in a cycle of blame of self and others, keeping our value low and therefore continuing the cycle of low self-esteem. Forgiveness can be challenging, and it does not make the other people/person right or excuse their behaviour, but it frees us from carrying the burden of that experience.

WORKSHEET

How to begin to forgive –

Begin to reduce your standards for others.

What are your standards? Do others need to meet these?

What can you do differently?

Understanding differences in values. What are your values?

Are you expecting everyone to have the same?

What changes would you like to make?

How can you show compassion and begin to see things through other people's eyes?

What will you need to do for this to happen?

Do you often find yourself blaming others?

How can you make sense of the above and what do you need to do differently?

Have compassion for the experiences/circumstances of others at that time.

How can you have compassion for others?

What might you need to do to see things from other people's perspective?

WORKSHEET

Give yourself time to think about people towards whom you hold anger or resentment.

How is this impacting on you?

Can you feel the impact on your body?

Do you feel you can let go of them?

Would you like to let go of them?

Now plan to start ...

WORKSHEET

Who would you like to forgive?

Do you remember why you were angry/resentful in the first place?

Is there any reason you need to hold on to these feelings?

If you let them go, how might you feel?

Forgiveness is a part of recovery and healing. How can you begin to start your own process?

Now plan your action ...

Gratitude

Appreciating positive experiences in life can improve our self-worth, help build/strengthen our social bonds and reduce low mood as not taking things for granted and appreciating what we have means we have less tendency to dwell on past events, which in turn reduces negative emotions of bitterness, greed, and anger. Encouraging behaviour that is productive, providing effective ways to reduce stress and therefore being more positive in life and towards others.

I call it 'Gratitude not Attitude'.

Gratitude journals are also useful tools to appreciate what we have rather than focus on what we do not have. Helping others in greater need allows our esteem to grow and increases the value of our own lives as there is always someone worse off than us. Spending time in nature appreciating our surroundings can also improve our overall sense of wellbeing. Appreciating the positive things in our lives rather than focusing on the negatives.

Gratitude is essential for a healthy, happy life; appreciating the things we have at home, like comforts, food, love, warmth, etc.

Not always having had all of the above in my life has made it easier for me to be grateful for them; however, I do not feel we need to lose things to appreciate them. I have had experience of having no food and the feeling of hunger. I have had lots of negative experiences in life; however, I have also had lots of positive experiences, which is what I choose to focus on and choose to be grateful for.

Gratitude for me is a way of being. Listening to the birds sing in the morning makes me smile; choosing what I would like to cook for dinner makes me feel I care about me and choose to care about me. Looking into a child's eyes and seeing the wonder of life, hearing the questioning and amazement makes me smile and really appreciate all that is.

Feeling like I am helping others see their full potential allows me to feel grateful and appreciate the life I have. 'Just being' and knowing that I have choices every day is sometimes enough. Yes, people may think it is a cliché; however, having had my life experiences, I can honestly say it can be this way when you have come from nothing and had nothing, then it matters more to appreciate things when you have them. I do not think it is just my generation as there is poverty/ deprivation throughout the world today. I just see it for me today as more of a state of mind.

WORKSHEET

Being grateful can be a challenge for most humans; it is something we find hard to think about. I ask as part of your self-care and esteem to really think about things/ways you can show your gratitude today. Even if you feel you do not have anything to be grateful for, there is always at least one thing. Examples: life, health, physical appearance, friends, family, job, etc.

Take some time to think about the things that you are grateful for and begin to write them down.

Think of three things you are grateful for today.

Was there a time when you did not feel grateful? If so, why?

How can you fully bring gratitude to your life?

What is your plan ...?

Bringing gratitude into your life ...

My plan of Gratitude is ...

Chapter Seventeen

OLIVER'S JOURNEY
(Oliver–male, forties)

What makes a happily married man with children seek the services of an escort?

I thought I knew the answer to this question. I had, after all, been taught it at home, school, within my faith community and through the media. Such a man was obviously a weak-minded fool who was unable to control his primal urges and would become the agent of his own destruction.

My belief made it even more terrifying when I found myself in this very situation. In fact, I was seeking the services of a male escort.

While I believed the desire to be wrong and recognised the destruction that could accompany it, the urge was overwhelming. There was a moment when even the prospect of losing my wife and children was not enough to deter me, and it was at this point that I recognised I needed help.

At my first counselling session with Susan, I had a clear objective in mind: I needed her to obliterate the desire and, if she could not do that, I needed her help to repress the urges.

The first thing that surprised me was that Susan did not share my sense of moral outrage at how I was feeling. Instead, without any sense of judgement, she encouraged me to explore what I was feeling and why. In doing so, we explored my relationship with my wife and children as well as relationships with other family and friends.

This exploration took me back to the experiences that formed my understanding of physical relationships. Most of my childhood was spent in a Catholic single-sex boarding school where I was taught that any form of sexual expression was sinful. Having sex to produce children was permissible, but priests, by resisting sex altogether, were clearly closer to God.

Having never experienced sexual intimacy with another person, I accepted I would remain single and developed an independent, isolated lifestyle. I never expected to meet and fall in love with my wife, let alone to marry and have children. Nevertheless, I had many unresolved issues which became impossible to ignore.

Over months of counselling, I discovered two important things:

Firstly, my feelings are part of who I am, and it is destructive to repress or deny them. My guilt and shame only intensified the feelings I was ashamed of, and this created a vicious circle. Through my counselling, I found the freedom to recognise and respect the full spectrum of feelings I experience without having to restrict myself to a particular label and without punishing myself for how I feel. In doing so, I felt a release from a heavy weight that I had been carrying for so long that it never occurred to me I could put it down.

Secondly, I am free to make my own decisions. Susan challenged me to consider what I really wanted out of life and what I wanted my future to look like. Her biggest question to me was whether I wanted to remain with my wife. I had never asked myself this question because I had promised to remain married for life and meant it. While this sense of duty has its place, it is not enough by itself to maintain a healthy relationship. Over time, I was able to appreciate the love that my wife and I have for each other, imperfect though it is, and to celebrate that this relationship is the most important thing in my life.

This summary does not do justice to the full rollercoaster of emotions I experienced over the months of counselling, as I explored different scenarios of what my future might look like and came to terms with who I am. Susan did not remove the part of me I struggled with, but she did help me to recognise, accept and love myself in my entirety. This has had a profound effect on me: I am less burdened by my imperfections and, for the first time, treat my whole self with care, respect and love. My wife and I have become closer and, while we still have challenges ahead of us, we share a passion to continue supporting each other on life's journey. Furthermore, having broken the cycle of overwhelming guilt and inadequacy, my relationship with my children has improved; I am pleased to say that our home has a lot more laughter and fewer regulations!

What makes a happily married man with children seek the services of an escort?

I have learnt that this question cannot be answered with labels and condemnations. Answering this question through counselling takes longer and is more challenging, but the effect is life-changing.

Working alliance

When I first began collaborating with Oliver, I noted very early on how his dialogue about himself was rather negative and self-critical. I noted a lack of nurturing, including a heaviness of shame that appeared when talking about his childhood experiences. He was a very likeable chap; polite and respectful. I noted this as something of value as I appreciated his politeness and respect as well as his value of the space on offer.

It was very evident that he loved his wife/family and wanted things to work out. He initially wanted me to remove this behaviour from him and I informed him that there was no magic wand, but we could explore the behaviour within his counselling, and I reassured him that I would be on the journey with him. I offered the client a safe space, respect, a working alliance and understanding for his situation without judgement but with empathy and compassion for his experiences.

He talked about his experience of boarding school from an early age, and he acknowledged that this was where he received his learning for intimacy (or lack of), social skills/management of feelings, sex education and acceptable behaviour. The client explained that his techniques to survive were focusing solely on his learning to fit in and be the best student.

He was not initially aware that his experiences may appear as abusive by others, stating that the teachers and priests had normalised them. Once explored, the client could recognise that some behaviours experienced by the children/boys from priests were not appropriate nor were they healthy.

Once the client understood that he had choices, he began to practise strategies to raise his self-esteem, to understand his behaviours and acknowledge the impact of his past experiences on the here and now. He focused on intimacy with his wife, internal dialogue, the relationship with his children, nurturing himself and building new ways of being within these relationships.

He began to experiment on new things to improve himself and his relationships, acknowledging that some of the learning had not been useful for him as it had not given him the tools he needed for growth. He gained an understanding of what he had felt was lacking, i.e., boundaries, self-esteem and intimacy, which initially he felt may have been distorted. He reduced then stopped unhelpful behaviours, implementing new ways of nurturing instead.

Oliver is both intelligent and successful within his career of choice, and had the confidence to maintain his position within his field. He had real depth of character, was open, willing to try new things, implement changes, some of which were challenging, and he was honest within this entire process. His honesty, good manners, willingness to change and challenge himself was for me to be not only respected but valued. A kind man who had not experienced a lot of love but who was willing to make changes so that he could find the love he needed, not only for himself but also for his family.

CHAPTER EIGHTEEN

SHAME AND ITS IMPACT ON SELF-ESTEEM

The function of shame

- The gaze and scrutiny of others ...
- Regulates prosocial behaviour, empathy, compassion ...
- Inclusion vs Exclusion ...
- Visibility vs Invisibility ...
- Comparison and judgement ...
- Status, power, honour ...
- Control over body, behaviour, others ...
- Cultural factors ...

The impact of shame

- **Loss of self** – inadequacy, defectiveness, narcissistic wounds ...
- **Loss of healthy pride** – spontaneity, pleasure, feeling fraudulent ...
- **Loss of agency** – self-efficacy, potency ...
- **Existential angst** – invisibility, exclusion ...
- **Relational hunger** – connection, belongingness ...
- **Disavowed shame** – shadow, defences against shame, grandiosity, hubristic pride, shamelessness, rage, violence, addictions ...

Comparison and competition

- **Expectations** – self and others ...
- **Perfectionism and insatiability** - a need to get everything right all the time, an appetite to achieve, driven to excel to own detriment ...

Defences against shame

- **Withdrawal** – hide, appeasement, compliance, submission ...
- **Attack self** – self-deprecation, self-harm, self-destructive behaviour ...
- **Avoidance** – disavowed shame, perfectionism, grandiosity, narcissism, addictions, thrill seeking, entitlement ...
- Attack other – shame or humiliate others, 'shamelessness', eroticised rage, violence, sexual violence ...

Research shows that babies do not feel shame as this does not develop until the age of around two years. When a child becomes a toddler, the child experiences shame to inhibit potentially dangerous situations as a way of grown-ups keeping the child safe and in their control. Often, parents use shaming to control their children to behave, be quiet, sit still as they learnt that way themselves. Shame feels personal, 'about me', shamed for making mistakes, speaking up, being happy, being proud, showing individuality, not doing as we were told to do. Parents may disallow their child to separate and explore itself, setting unhealthy boundaries that finally solidify into the parents modelling and demanding that the child/parent boundaries be rigid or too loose. By the age of two years, the child is already becoming moulded into a distortion of this potential to learn about otherwise unhealthy differences, into toxic shame and low self-esteem internalised, stifling the child's healthy exploration and creativity.

Feeling shamed usually relates to a boundary problem, and a 'never' response may indicate a lack of awareness of feelings. As described, the feelings of shame in the healing child within is a painful feeling that adult children and co-dependents experience frequently growing up. All shame is unnecessary; it serves us no purpose. What shame suggests is that we are somehow inadequate or not good enough. It is related to several core issues, especially being real with one's own feelings and low self-esteem. Shame and over-responsibility for others, becoming embarrassed (feeling ashamed in the presence of one other person) when another person acts up, is usually an indication of boundaries being too loose.

Shame is more common in people that have experienced oppression by society, living in poverty, seen as different. Working classes not being as good, difference including ethnicity, identity, sexuality, etc., can lead to shame, culture-facilitating compliance, seen not heard, strong emphasis on what is seen as good behaviour, fear or shame; the quickest way to get children to be compliant, to do what you want, etc. Feeling shamed by lack of eye contact, looking down, away from, certain behaviours of passing the message of shame from parent to child and culture to culture.

Different ethnic communities affected by racial violence, racism, have experience of this by being treated as less than, experiencing visual negative responses leading to anxiety, discomfort, chronic compliance and repetitive patterns of behaviour trying to fit in. Shame is a complex and entrenched issue, which leads to people building their own defence mechanisms to feel safe/protected. Shame accompanied by abuse or neglect compounds the message that you are not being good enough. The survival responses can be to look away, look down, to be submissive, which can appear as more common in the oppressed.

My experience of growing up in the sixties and seventies; there was a greater tendency for males to get angry and for society to be more tolerant, more likely to accept outbursts from little boys than little girls. Historically, women in the western world have been taught how to be more compliant, shamed for expressing self or speaking up, having a voice. Shame strategy to de-escalate situations can be related to appeasement, damage limitation, head down, no eye contact, faint voice, etc. (survival)

When I first thought of writing a chapter on shame and self-esteem, I initially appeared to struggle with the subject matter. I started to think about the feelings of shame I carried, and even thinking about it made me feel as though for a short while I was back there reliving the shame I felt as a young person/sometimes as a child. It saddened me to think of my younger self carrying the burden of shame.

I knew what shame was from an early age and going to Catholic church and Sunday school as the word was a constant reminder of how we had been conditioned to be and feel. Even the language back in the sixties and seventies was very much based around shame. 'You should be ashamed of yourself.' If you showed any individuality or difference in your thinking or did not conform to society's views, then you would experience feeling shamed for this. So, as a child, I conformed; I would do what I was told to do by adults, acting accordingly, whatever that meant. My initial schooling appeared to go well. I believe my reports would state that I was a good child, quiet, shy, although melancholic too.

It was not until my teens that I really began to express myself by changing my name, finding my fashion/colours, whether it be dying my hair or wearing red nail polish and lipstick. There was shame or shaming when women/girls wore the colour red as it was associated with sex or not being innocent! The red lipstick and nail polish for me was the glamour from the 1940s movies. I loved Bette Davis and Joan Crawford movies; they were strong female role models for me, and I loved the glamour of the red as I felt it to be powerful, although probably did not understand it at that time. It frustrated me when I received comments about wearing red deemed as inappropriate, connecting the colour to sex, sex work, negative images of females, etc. I felt as a young person that the labels were sexualising children and not valuing the expression of the young. Shaming each other for being who we are, how we are, not allowing the person to grow or be creative in their expression of self, the freedom of expression, whether it be sexuality, gender, race, non-binary, beliefs, musical interests, creativity, etc.

One of the most frequent problematic feelings with low self-esteem is shame. Why would anyone want to treat us badly and possibly abandon us unless we are somehow inadequate or bad? So, when a person leaves, without a healthy self, healthy boundaries, we may feel not only inordinate amounts of shame, but we may also be vulnerable to taking on and absorbing the other person's projected shame, which is not ours. With very few or sometimes no healthy role models, and with a repeated sense of invalidation, rejection, feeling of fear, shame and other emotional pain, this may end up being the core issue of difficulty when handling feelings in general. With overly rigid boundaries of keeping feelings in, and overly loose ones of letting in others' painful feelings that are not yours, you may end up feeling numb, which is an empty and painful absence of feeling anything. Often feeling that the other person will abandon you, and with low self-esteem and shame, we are now more susceptible to getting wounded around several other core issues, inappropriate behaviour, and may have difficulty trusting others.

Shame affects us all differently; shame can be not feeling accepted as they are but feeling that there is a need or expectation to look a certain way, behave a certain way. Many women have experienced shaming for being what might be described as overly emotional, when going through changes in hormones. Men can feel shamed into not allowing their vulnerability and preventing them showing their true emotions, not allowing them to seek mental health care despite them having high suicide rates. Men are at times shamed, expected to behave in a manner that is projected on to them with what is believed to be their role in society. We may feel shamed around our ethnicity, our sex lives, our sexuality, or being a part of the LGBTQIA+ community; we all have our own stigmas of shame attached to us. Not regarding oneself as male or female in today's society, made to feel shame for this rather than society accepting people just as they are. Each story of shame affects our self-worth and gives us the message that we are not okay just as we are. Acceptance of our humanness, whatever that means to the individual!

When we start to translate the shame into our later lives, we may see how we may start to avoid shame. We might try to numb our shame, with addictions, debt, gambling and violence, etc. (all issues which are psychologically related to shame) Alternatively, we may try to perfect ourselves to meet the ideals we feel we need to so we can stay as far away from shame as possible. We might do this through 'correcting' what shames us, going through procedures of cosmetic surgery to change physically and to hide or cover what we regard as defects. We may spend money on things we cannot afford or show a face of confidence to the world to avoid the deep-seated discomfort we have with ourselves. These are just some of the ways we keep our low self-esteem at bay, by trying to manufacture what looks like high self-esteem but which in turn fuels our shame.

Wherever we are born, we inherit generations of ideas, beliefs and behaviour from family, culture, religion and society, and through this process are given certain messages over time. Our emotions are based on aspects of our social location, gender, age, class, race, etc.

In the western world, we are systematically trained to suppress our emotions. The impact of this can be felt by deadening our vitality in shame, depression and anxiety, all prevalent in modern society, and our inability to manage our emotions in relation to others.

Asserting self – making a request is about finding a way to meet our needs. By asking, we acknowledge our interdependence, which can open us up to disappointment or rejection. Experience has taught us that it is dangerous, shameful or futile, leading us to not bother, not doing, not asking. We may also learn that giving to others is a way to get our needs met, that help from another can only be laced with hidden agendas. Our ability to say 'no' is a sign of a healthy relationship. 'Yes' often comes from an unhealthy place of fear, shame or obligation.

People feel shame for lots of reasons: too tall, too short, poverty, rape survivor, cancer survivor, etc. People feel shame for many things they have no control over, and for which they have no responsibility. (Shame is not exclusive.)

Shame is what we feel when we fall short of our own or other people's expectations, when we feel responsible for being morally inadequate. It is a discombobulation at the level of identity, 'not comfortable in our own skin'. Shame is a manifestation of existential dissonance.

Having an alcoholic father for me was one point of my shame. Denial of his behaviour and acceptance of this being the norm as that was my experience within the community in which I lived. Although my father had a respectable job and was known to be intelligent and fortunate within his career, he spent all of his earnings in the betting shop and down the pub, so others' view of him and the reality of his behaviour were vastly different. Also, just like in today's society, it was a case of showing one picture to society while another was behind closed doors.

I repeated many behaviours that I learnt and also became a perfectionist to cover my shame. Working to the extreme to prove my self-worth, doing more for others than self, drinking to access (teens/twenties), using food as a tool to self-soothe or punish, spending money, especially in my twenties, that I did not have, buying things I did not need and generally trying to hide my shame.

Sorting out and letting go of what does not belong to us is often easier than sorting or owning what does. Paradoxically, to do this letting go takes a firm background in learning to sort out and take responsibility for what is actually ours. Having healthy boundaries is a crucial part of this process.

At the centre of what is most affected by shame is our self-esteem, because the world teaches us that if we are not a certain way then we are not good enough or deserving. When this feeling sets in, it can pierce our self-worth and our self-perception. Yet if we leave shame unattended and continue to avoid it, it often sneaks its way into our lives unconsciously. We cannot selectively choose to not feel certain emotions; if we try to cut off from one, we cut off from many, including the good feelings of joy, gratitude, purpose and belonging.

It is through shame and being able to separate that from our identity that we can embrace our value. When we raise our self-esteem, we learn belonging, kindness, compassion, empathy, love. We are more open to people and opportunities that are good for us and can embrace them without fear and insecurity. Most importantly, we learn that we are enough just the way we are.

WORKSHEET

Answer the following questions as honestly as you can.

What does shame mean to you?

How do you recognise shame?

How do you link your poor self-esteem with shame?

How does shame impact on your life?

How does shame affect your relationships with others?

How do you prevent yourself from entering a low self-esteem spiral and triggering shame?

What can you do to reduce your level of shame?

Write down three examples of feeling shame.
1.

2.

3.

How did it affect you?

How did you behave?

What will you do differently now that you have completed the above?

WORKSHEET

Give yourself some time to think about the word shame and what it means to you.

Think about times in your life when you have felt shame and what the consequences were for you. Also, think about times in your life when others have made you feel shame and what happened.

Do you feel shame?

If so, what do you feel shame over?

Do you feel you need to continue to carry your shame? If so, why?

When exploring shame, do you feel that it has been something that was given to you rather than something you own yourself?

Think about a time when you have felt shame. What would you like to say to yourself about it today?

How can you begin to release shame from your life?

What steps will you take to begin this process?

CHAPTER NINETEEN

JACK'S JOURNEY
(Jack–male, early twenties)

Jack came to see me due to having anxiety and negative self-talk, wanting to achieve his goals but lacking belief in himself. Jack was in recovery of an eating disorder and was slowly coming to terms with the impact it had had on his life and his relationships. Jack presented as a well-mannered, intelligent young man with good family links and values. He appeared mature and put this down to his parental guidance (diligent parents with strong values). When I collaborated with Jack, he appeared motivated and willing to make changes and, in some sense, appeared in a rush to get there. I acknowledged this and discussed in the sessions whereby Jack owned up to having a perfectionist driven attitude towards life which was both positive and negative for him. This need to get there and for all to be perfect was something we returned to several times within his therapy. Jack talked about his lack of worth and needing to build his esteem but found this difficult due to his negative self-talk. Like many, Jack often ruminated in his thoughts, which led to increased anxiety and reduced esteem. We explored several ways of being both creative and structured within the sessions. There were times when we worked together in a space and other times when we worked online. Jack stated he noticed the difference online and preferred face-to-face work as he felt it benefitted him more.

Jack used the space to talk about the expectations of society, social media, comparing self to others and his generation's wants/needs. We explored this at length, working together to challenge some of this thinking, and began to make a pathway that worked for him. Jack was very much a thinker and liked evidence-based work, so we explored ways to increase his worth and reduce his inner critic by making minor changes to his lifestyle. Jack acknowledged that structure was the most important thing for him to enable change, so we built a pathway of simple steps of structure, including balanced exercise routine, healthy relationships with food, self-care plan, social activities, relationships with friends/family, work/life balance, meditation space, mindfulness living, recognising and understanding repetitive cycles of behaviour and thoughts.

We worked through each step as Jack built them into his life as well as referencing the changes he had made to date and pausing to look back to acknowledge them as this reinforced his ability and motivation to continue to change. Jack began to balance his work/life/exercise and prioritise his self-care, finding a balance that suited him and which did not increase his anxiety but was manageable to continue a healthier way of being instead of the previous extremes. He built a pathway that was structured and kind, recognising his needs first and prioritising his wellbeing. After some time of us working together, Jack moved from weekly sessions to fortnightly, then monthly then every other month, enabling him to gradually work through his pathway, acknowledging his independence to achieve set goals as well as assessing himself on his journey and feeding back what he felt he still needed, and where the pathway needed to go.

We were always mindful of Jack's previous eating disorder and his recovery, which was something we came back to many times to ensure that I was not enabling this nor was I colluding in any way with any destructive behaviours. We also talked honestly about his perfectionist side of self – ensuring that we worked safely and honestly with all of the above in a partnership that prioritised Jack's ongoing recovery in a safe, effective way.

Jack works in an environment that is fast paced so can often be perceived as not encouraging good self-care, and he is also studying at university, which we took into consideration when planning and implementing his pathway. Time taken to consider his needs, the safety of the environment in which he works, as well as ongoing learning within the therapeutic relationship. I showed Jack my humanness, allowing myself to make mistakes as well as showing him my humour in an appropriate way.

Our relationship began slowly from scratch as respectful, approachable and trusting. Jack allowed me to see him clearly over time by his openness and willingness to trust in the therapeutic process. I appreciated his willingness, his ability to be open to the challenges of therapy and his honesty throughout the journey, which allowed him space to grow and continue to do so. I gained insight into what it was like being a young male in society today and how this pressure felt as well as having such an impact on the value of oneself. Jack reminded me of differences within his generation and to not be so presumptuous regarding this, acknowledging my recognition of not becoming Mother in the alliance. I was aware that the above did not happen and this was due to him being what I experienced as an old soul (respectfully intended). His willingness and openness throughout our journey together enabled him to make lots of positive changes which he stated have improved his life, his relationships, growing independently in confidence within these relationships and work as well as in general life.

Jack's review of therapy

Due to past therapy, I understood that I am more comfortable with female therapists, and this was something I actively sought when looking to start counselling sessions. This was reaffirmed to me within the first few sessions as I felt at ease with Susan, and I was able to build a trusting relationship quickly. This may also have been helped by my willingness to be open and to get to and understand the root problem I was experiencing.

Susan's understanding and experience were also something that I found comforting and added to the level of trust. Susan having much more exposure not only to mindfulness but also general life experiences meant that I was able to take each session as a learning curve, which served my inquisitive nature well, aiding my growth.

Chapter Twenty

HELEN'S JOURNEY
(Helen–female, thirties)

Sitting there at my home desk, I could see my laptop screen flashing, but my vision had become so blurry it looked like a haze of lights. I blinked several times to see if my vision cleared but it just stayed the same. My head was full of questions, to-dos, conversations with my manager, my team, and I felt frantic and full of dread. Work always consumed my thoughts but in that particularly scary moment, the only words I could muster up the courage to speak were to my husband, panicked words: 'I can't carry on like this. I feel like I'm losing my mind.'

This episode wasn't the first red flag to me, but it was the one where I started to take things more seriously and led me to contact Susan for help. I remember thinking I'm sure six sessions will do the trick. There is just something wrong with me and Susan will see what it is straight away. I need to try harder; I need more time management. Nothing could be further from the truth. I'd spent most of my life being a 'tryer' with a capital T. Endless people-pleasing, lack of any kind of boundaries and incredibly low self-esteem contributed to my burnout.

Susan started by asking me to do one nice thing for myself every day, indulge in something I fancied. My mind drew a blank. I used to love having a bath, but even a bath would conjure up all sorts of work-related thinking and endless to-do lists. What did I like doing? I had no idea anymore. My identity revolved around pleasing other people, and this was particularly rewarded well at work with promotions and pay rises. 'You're smashing it' was regularly texted/emailed to me by my boss alongside a list of new things to do, which I eagerly agreed to every time.

It has been a long and slow healing journey for me. With the incredible support of Susan holding my hand all the way, I began to understand who I am and what I want while unpicking incredibly painful experiences. For the first time, I was listening to myself. All the answers to the questions I had were within me; I had just never listened to myself before. I used to see assertiveness as 'bullying'. However, now I see it as necessary.

And the biggest secret to all of this? Loving myself. Something I had heard many times scrolling through social media, but until I had gone through the process of unpicking how and why I was living my life, I didn't realise how fundamental this was to my happiness.

Working alliance

Working with Helen in the first few weeks was about building the relationship and gaining an understanding of her way of thinking as well as exploring the need to please within this. I was aware of the need to go gently with the subject of taking time for self, as Helen appeared to struggle with the concept of slowing down and what that might mean for her. There appeared to be a need being met by the trying hard and doing, with negative consequences for herself and her family. We unpicked how her life might be different and what that would mean to her as well as how exploring your inner dialogue to achieve gave a person value. It was a road that we walked at a gentle pace, me being mindful of the history of the person in front of me and her need to get things right as well as please me. Helen initially wanted to take away some tools to practise within a six-week timeframe; however, as we worked together, this changed and she became aware that more time was needed for her to gain as much as possible from the sessions as well as the time needed to build the relationship with me. Most of our work together was about Helen taking the time for herself and allowing herself to relax and have some fun without feeling as though she needs to perform for others. Also, recognising her abilities, self-love, self-worth and forgiveness, especially for her past experiences and the impact they have had on her up until now. Helen initially worked hard within the sessions, which was recognised as a behavioural pattern to please, then we changed tactics to explore doing things differently, and what I call 'the light bulb moment' came. Helen began to realise that she did not need to please me to be liked, nor did she need to perform or try to make me laugh. We built a relationship as two women, equal listening and learning, making small changes each step of the way. I saw the child that had not felt heard or guided with love. Helen showed me her true self and trusted in the process of therapy. I valued her ability to be honest and to be challenged within the setting even though it was tough at times. She is an amazing woman and mother who does her absolute best in whatever she undertakes and through this learning was able to ditch the perfect and be good enough!

ACKNOWLEDGEMENTS

Keith – my husband, who has been by my side for the past twenty plus years, is always supporting me in whatever project or plan I have undertaken or wanted to undertake, always believing in me and being my biggest fan. You have brought so much sunshine, laughter, love and appreciation into my life. Equality, feminism, punk, politics, our values, our love, value of all life, the ability to believe that we all have a purpose and a place in the world, no matter what our experiences. With love x

Avis – my sister in-law who sadly died on 31st October 2012. She was my guiding light; my compass; my teacher; a constant, consistent figure, especially in my early years. We shared a connection and love that I will always cherish. A woman, a mother with a strong faith and ability to be her authentic self, no matter who she was with. Avis showed me how a black woman in the 1970s through all her negative experiences could still show so much love and kindness to others, no matter who they were or what they had done. She came into my life at the crucial time of puberty, when I needed a role model, and I will always remember her with love.

Mother – I have not always understood your decision-making, nor have I always appreciated you; however, through the tough times, the sad times and the mad times, I have known that you have tried your best when taking into consideration your own experiences of life. You are a strong, formidable woman who has survived immense suffering, and yet you still have an amazing fight, drive and spirit that I will always value and cherish. I love you x

With appreciation and thanks to **Mandie ... and others who will remain anonymous.** Thank you for allowing me to use your experiences within this book. You have all come a long way and worked extremely hard to get where you are today. Thank you for choosing me to join you on your journey.

For every page I write, I reflect and remember the people I have worked with over the years and their journeys. I have gained so much from each relationship. I value the gift of being human, collaborating with other humans, with all our complexities and imperfections. Being who we are in that moment as much as we can be within the boundaries of therapy. I think as therapists we do fill a space/role (s), consciously or unconsciously, to enable clients to grow/change/heal.

THE PURPLE BUTTERFLY

The purple butterfly was someone who came into my life and sadly left this earth too early. She had such a profound impact that I will carry her forever in my heart.

The purple butterfly was born into a family that lacked boundaries and safety. She was unaware of the consequences and how they would always be to her detriment as well as negatively impact her self-esteem.

Her relationships were abusive and destructive, which just compounded her previous experience and trauma repeatedly. She longed for a love story, one that would keep her safe, enable her to have the life she so craved and deserved. To be herself, accepted for who she was and how she was, a hero to protect her vulnerability and love her, no matter what. What she received was nothing like what she deserved, and this was due to her lack of value of herself. We can create our own self-fulfilling prophecy by how we show ourselves to the world and what we attract.

The purple butterfly was an amazing woman, full of life, fun and laughter. However, there was a deep sadness, a trauma that she carried with her until her last breath. If only I could have helped her heal from the pain and hurt she carried, but no one could have made her feel what she could not, nor could anyone make her see the qualities she had.

Some people come into our lives for short periods of time but touch our hearts so deeply that they leave their mark and stay. She gave me an opportunity to see what kind of mother I might be, the freedom to show all of me and not feel judged. She allowed me to find my Hippie Chic, who I have always had but sometimes kept a secret. She showed me how to just be who I am, not continue to conform or be what others expected me to be. She was the purple butterfly who will live forever fluttering freely, no longer trapped in the trauma of her past but free to be exactly who she is/was without the fear, anger and pain of the past. Go free, purple butterfly, and live your life the way it was meant to be.

In Loving Memory of a Fiery, Passionate, Gentle, Kind woman who lived a brief time but made her mark. Always in my heart x

References and support

Louise Hay – Having read You Can Heal Your Life in 1993, this was the beginning of my journey to find the core of me. This started the process of realising I am not my labels, nor am I my experiences. Louise Hay helped me see things differently, sharing her experiences and allowing others to know her journey within her own healing.

Charles L Whitfield, MD – Boundaries and Relationships, 1993. Knowing, protecting and enjoying the self. Checking out our boundaries in relationships and knowing our limits. I used the survey from this book as I felt it would be useful for readers to understand their boundaries within relationships and as an understanding of what, if anything, one needs to change.

Melanie Fennell – Overcoming Low Self-esteem. Reading this book in 2004, and using some of the text in Shine Your Light, enabled me to not only gain a better understanding of low self-esteem and the impact on my life but also the impact on the clients I worked with and how to support change.

Patrick Holford – Optimum Nutrition for the Mind. An amazing book to explore the impact of nutrition on the brain. This book has been so helpful for me to have a better understanding of nutrition and its impact on mental health. It is a subject I have been interested in for a few years, which led me to get a diploma in nutrition to help myself, my family and the clients I work with.

Ed Halliwell – Into the Heart of Mindfulness. This amazing book takes you on a step-by-step journey into mindfulness and a man's journey of healing. I have recommended this book to many of my clients, especially as a useful tool for anxiety and depression.

References

Whitfield, L Charles, MD, Boundaries and Relationships (1993). Health communications, inc. Florida USA.

Fennell, Melanie, Overcoming Low Self-esteem (1999). Robinson Publishing Ltd.

Halliwell, Ed, Into the Heart of Mindfulness (2016). Piatkus London.